THE ROAD TO HOLINESS

*Dedicated to
Ken Collins and Mark Butlin,
whose gifts of discernment
have helped me along the road
of discipleship.*

SEAN CONNOLLY

The Road to Holiness

Reflections on discipleship

ST PAULS

ST PAULS Publishing
Morpeth Terrace, London SW1P 1EP, UK

Copyright © ST PAULS 1999

ISBN 085439 573 3

Set by TuKan, High Wycombe
Produced in the EC
Printed by Interprint Ltd., Marsa, Malta

ST PAULS is an activity of the priests and brothers
of the Society of St Paul who proclaim the Gospel
through the media of social communication

ACKNOWLEDGEMENTS

All Scripture quotations, unless otherwise noted, are taken from the New Jerusalem Bible, published in the United Kingdom by Darton, Longman & Todd, Ltd., © 1985. Used with permission.

Permission has been kindly granted to the author to reprint excerpts from the following publications:

G. Hughes, *Knocking on Heaven's Door* published in The Tablet, 21 February 1998. © 1998 by The Tablet Publishing Company Ltd., 1 King Street Cloisters, Clifton Walk, London W6 0QZ.

(ed.), T. Fry O.S.B., *The Rule of St Benedict in English*, The Liturgical Press, Collegeville, Minnesota, U.S.A., 1982. © 1981 by the Order of St Benedict, Inc., Collegeville, Minnesota, U.S.A.

K. Collins, *The Prayer of Jesus*, in *The Unsealed Fountain*, Oscott Series 1. © First Published by Veritas Publications, 7-8 Lower Abbey Street, Dublin 1, Ireland. Used with permission.

G. Holzherr, *The Rule of Benedict. A Guide to Christian Living*, translated by Monks of Glenstal Abbey, published by Four Courts Press Ltd., Fumbally Lane, Dublin 8, Ireland, 1994. © 1994 Glenstal Abbey.

C. S. Lewis, *The Great Divorce*, HarperCollins Publishers Ltd., 77-85 Fulham Palace Road, Hammersmith, London W6 8JB. © 1946 by C. S. Lewis.

C. Martini, (trans. Susan Leslie), *Ministers of the Gospel. Meditations on St Luke's Gospel*, © 1983 St Paul's Publishing, Morpeth Terrace, Victoria, London SW1P 1EP.

J. Sobrino, (trans. P. Burns & F. McDonagh), *Jesus the Liberator. A Historical-Theological Reading of Jesus of Nazareth*, © 1993 by Orbis Books, published in 1994 by Burns & Oates, Wellwood, North Farm Road, Tunbridge Wells, Kent TN2 3DR. Used with permission of Burns & Oates.

J. M. Crum, *Now the Green Blade Riseth*, © Oxford University Press, Great Clarendon Street, Oxford OX2 6DP. Used with permission.

Julian of Norwich, (trans. C. Wolters), *Revelations of Divine Love*, published by Penguin Classics, 1985. © 1966 by Clifton Wolters. Used with permission of Penguin UK, 27 Wrights Lane, London W8 5TZ.

D. Ross, *Interview with Dr. Jonathan Sacks*, published in The Independent on 4 May 1998. © 1998 by Independent Newspapers (UK) Ltd., 1 Canada Square, Canary Wharf, London E14 5DL. Used with permission.

T. Sutcliffe, *Television Review*, published in The Independent on 21 April 1998. © 1998 by Independent Newspapers (UK) Ltd., 1 Canada Square, Canary Wharf, London E14 5DL. Used with permission.

(Trans., J. Beevers), *The Autobiography of St Thérèse of Lisieux. The Story of a Soul.* © 1957 by Doubleday, a division of Bantam Doubleday Dell Publishing Group, Inc., 1540 Broadway, New York, New York 10036, U.S.A.

Bishops' Conference of England & Wales, *The Sign We Give*. Report from the working party on collaborative ministry, published by Matthew James Publishing Ltd., 19 Wellington Close, Chelmsford, Essex, CM1 2EE. © 1995 Bishops' Conference of England and Wales.

St Augustine, (trans., B. Ulanov), *On the Psalms, 102, 3*, published in B. Ulanov, *Prayers of St Augustine*, Seabury Press, 430 Oak Grove, Minneapolis, Minnesota 55403, U.S.A. © 1983 Barry Ulanov. Used with the permission of the publisher.

Table of Contents

Foreword	9
Preface	11

Chapter One: The Meeting Place

Come and see	15
Tiredness	19
Encountering Christ	29
Irresistible love	36
Substitutes	40
Sin	46
Revelation	50

Chapter Two: The Way of Love

The sign we give	55
Humility	59
Understanding	64
Betrayal	68
Service	72

Chapter Three: The Cost of Discipleship

Inevitability	77
Compassion	82
Darkness	89
The last words	92
Sacred and profane	96

Chapter Four: The Call to Holiness

Come and eat	101
Seek the Lord	105
Stop and listen	109

Foreword

The Millennium is here. With our heads we can say, "It's only a number." But there is another part of us, quite another part, which has the sense of an era ending, and another dawning, a sense of something on the turn, something momentous.

It seems certain that the Church in our country must now find new ways of being, new ways of acting. The average age of the parish clergy is high, and there are not many men ready to take their place. The Catholic Church has survived in many places and at many times with few priests: no cause for panic. But it has to function in a new way. As far as we can see ahead (and that is not very far) the twenty-first century must be and will be the century of a sturdy, self-reliant laity.

For the people of our parishes to be this sort of people, they need a programme of personal prayer which is solid and durable, which can be returned to again and again. The word of God in the Bible is his gift to us all. The best prayer is prayer with Scripture, what the Benedictines call, *lectio divina*. If every Catholic knew how to take a gospel story and dwell with it, drawing the meaning from it, use it not so much for information as for communion with the living God, find in it the inspiration to love God and neighbour in a new way every day, then the face of the Church would be renewed.

Sean Connolly, with a deceptive simplicity, shows us how to do this. He shows us not so much how we must behave to be better Christians, but how the pages of Scripture reveal to us the face of a God who loves us deeply. Our first duty is not to transform our behaviour but to transform our way of being. We have to allow ourselves to be loved. The arm of the Lord is not shortened. He is still the Saviour who converted the woman at the well, who washed the disciples' feet, who was crucified and rose. He invites us – still – to the waters of life. This is a book which re-enkindles our faith and warms our hope.

Tony Philpot

Preface

Like many country places, some of the windy, narrow lanes and obscure trails of Norfolk are infuriatingly lacking in signposts. Or, if they do have signs, more often than not some wag of a local has twisted them around and has you going in circles.

The road to holiness, along which we must travel if we are serious about our discipleship of Christ, can often seem like one of those Norfolk roads. It will look to be too narrow to overtake, and so we cannot travel at the speed we would like. At times there appear sudden and unexpected bends, and we may wonder if we are going in the right direction at all. It is almost certainly potholed, making a smooth journey impossible. And as for clear signposts…? But for all this, there is the consolation that the road in these respects is pretty much the same for each of us. And we are not alone: we have one another, fellow travellers. More importantly, it is on this road that we encounter God. The road to holiness is not so much a journey somewhere, by which we map everything out, during which we work out all the directions. Rather, it is a process of encountering God and gradually letting him take over. With God, present and prompting, we gain the courage to follow the way of love, shown in the life of his Son, Jesus Christ. Inevitably having to count the cost of such love, we come to hear more clearly the call to abundant life: "Come to me; listen, and you will live."

This book began life as a collection of talks given to people in parishes and deaneries across East Anglia. They arose from my own personal *lectio divina* – that prayerful reading and rereading of Sacred Scripture. The aim was never exegesis, and I can never claim to be a scripture scholar. Rather they were offered as reflections taken from my own life of discipleship.

I am all too painfully aware that my own journey along the road to holiness has only just begun. I am only starting out, and yet already I have been helped by so many fellow disciples on the way. St Paul urged his communities to encourage one another. I am grateful that I have met more than my fair share of encouragement. My hope is that these reflections will encourage others to go on travelling and seeking holiness of life.

1
The Meeting Place

Reflections on the Woman at the Well
John 4:5-26

When our hearts are wintry, grieving or in pain,
thy touch can call us back to life again,
fields of our heart that dead and bare have been:
love is come again like wheat that springeth green.

(J. M. Crum 1872–1958)

Come and see

The next day as John stood there with two of his disciples, Jesus went past, and John looked towards him and said, "Look, there is the lamb of God." And the two disciples heard what he said and followed Jesus. Jesus turned round, saw them following and said, "What do you want?" They answered, "Rabbi," – which means Teacher – "where do you live?" He replied, "Come and see" (Jn 1:35-39).

Come and see – the basic invitation of Jesus to all who would be his disciples. The invitation to us as we begin our journey into the story of the woman at the well. In the above translation it is Jesus' response to the question, "What do you want?" The better translation is, "What do you seek?"[1] To those of us who seek holiness of life Jesus says, "Come and see".

Before we begin to look at John 4:5-26 it is worth spending some time reminding ourselves what leads up to it in John's Gospel. The Baptist, as we have seen, proclaims Jesus to be the Lamb of God and subsequently loses two of his disciples. Andrew, one of those two, drags his brother Simon along to meet the Lord with the promise, "We have found the Messiah." The next day Philip bumps into the Christ who is on his way to Galilee and is told, "Follow me." And what does Philip do? He finds

Nathanael and takes him to Jesus and it is Nathanael who declares: "Rabbi, you are the Son of God" (Jn 1:35-51).

If we jump a little to chapter three, we have Nicodemus, one of the Pharisees and a leader of the Jews, coming to Jesus under cover of night to tell him: "No one could perform the signs that you do unless God were with him" (Jn 3:1-2). We then have the account of Jesus' meeting with the Samaritan woman at the well and are told that many of the Samaritans of Sychar came to believe in him (Jn 4:39-42). And finally, at the end of the fourth chapter, we hear of Jesus curing the court official's son and how the whole of his household come to believe (Jn 4:46-53).

What is happening in this part of John's Gospel is that Jesus is gathering disciples – people are coming to believe in him. They may be Galilean fishermen, rather rough and uneducated. They may be followers of the Baptist, already used to the role of disciple. They may be flunkies of Herod's court, or Samaritans, or a Pharisee. What unites them all is their reaction to Jesus. Here is someone with something to offer. Let us come and see what he is about.

We also have as background to Jesus' journey into Samaria the gradual build up of another reaction: mistrust and suspicion. The miracle of the wedding feast at Cana is followed by the riotous scene where Jesus cleanses the Temple. The ministry of baptising in the Judaean countryside is marred by the rivalry of some of the Baptist's disciples. They complain to John, "the man to whom you bore witness is baptising now, and everyone is going to him."[2]

As there is a rag-bag of support growing for Jesus, so too there is a festering uncertainty and fear. How true is this situation even today? As Christians we live and minister in an imperfect environment, a sinful world. Sometimes we come across the suspicion and hostility of the outside world. Sometimes it strikes us just how far removed we are from their values. Think of the way soap operas parody Christian characters. Read any national newspaper and wonder at the duplicity of approach to the Church. Listen to the words of those men and women bearing witness to Christ in South America today, standing up to the evil of oppression:

The Latin American martyrs did die to defend the same cause as Jesus, God's kingdom for the poor, and they were threatened, persecuted and put to death by the anti-Kingdom.[3]

Sometimes the misunderstanding can simply be from ignorance or inherited prejudices. As a priest, I always smile to myself after a funeral when a non-Catholic will come up to me and pay the backhanded compliment: "Your service wasn't like anything we expected. It was quite nice really." Or the time I was asked by a barber, "So, what's the difference between you Catholics and them Christians then?" Indeed, what is the difference?

Sadly, for most of us, it can be friends and families where the misunderstanding is felt the most. Many of my family are not Christian and, although we love one another very much, every now and then I see the gulf between us. On certain subjects our thought processes are worlds apart. I see it too in parish life, having to be aware of wanting to involve someone more in the life of the parish but realising the strain that would put upon a marriage or a family.

We surround ourselves, then, in our Christian communities with support. We surround ourselves with people of like minds and like faith; but we too are a mixed bag. Whatever the official line, it is clear from talking to people how much we sometimes differ in the details of our faith. There are those of us like Nicodemus, fearful and unsure. Those of us like the Baptist's disciples, rather resentful with bruised egos. Most of us are just like the fishermen, getting it wrong time after time. In the end that doesn't matter. In the end Jesus takes us with him. In the end what is on offer is far greater than our imperfections; far greater than any hostility or opposition. The invitation still stands: come and see.

Tiredness

When Jesus heard that the Pharisees had found out that he was making and baptising more disciples than John – though in fact it was his disciples who baptised, not Jesus himself – he left Judaea and went back to Galilee. He had to pass through Samaria. On the way he came to the Samaritan town called Sychar near the land that Jacob gave to his son Joseph. Jacob's well was there and Jesus, tired by the journey, sat down by the well. It was about the sixth hour (Jn 4:1-6).

Jacob's well was situated at a cross-roads and the town of Sychar was probably about half a mile away. Jesus and his disciples were on their way back to Galilee from Judaea, having attracted some followers but having aroused notice and hostility, especially from the Jewish leaders and Temple officials. The cross-roads would have offered the choice of going into Samaria proper and on into western Galilee, where they were headed, or going north east towards the lake of Gennesaret.

What is significant for us is that Jesus is on a journey, Jesus is at a cross-roads, Jesus is in a foreign country, and that Jesus is tired. Some translations use the word, 'wearied'. We could say Jesus was exhausted – a sheer physical and mental fatigue. There is the journey and the heat. "It was about the sixth hour" means it was midday, with a burning sun overhead and little or no shelter. There is also the tension and hassle he had faced in Jerusalem and the surrounding Juadean countryside. Even the demands of those who supported him must have taken their toll.

We are used now to thinking of ourselves as the pilgrim people of God. What, then, of our journey? Where am I headed? Where am I coming from? Am I, like Jesus, leaving tension behind me? Is my involvement in the Church a flight from something? Am I running away? One of my great fears when I was preparing for priesthood was that I was fleeing from responsibility. Celibacy was not a challenge but a refuge. Ministry wasn't something that made sense of my life and forced me to grow in love but something I wanted on my own terms. In fact none of these fears turned out to be true, but the process of questioning was a valid one.

Last summer I went on holiday to the south of France with three friends. Each of us had been allocated jobs for the holiday. One was cook, one was translator, one was driver. I was the navigator. How proud I was of my maps and my pre-planned routes, my estimated times of arrival. How horribly wrong it all went when my three friends started interfering during the journey. "I'm sure there's a monastery around here somewhere, can we stop and have a look?" My response: "No, we're behind schedule already." "There's some beautiful sloping vineyards a couple of miles west of here, if we take the next exit." My response: "No, that's too slow, it's a country lane." At every turn I was out voted. And each time I had to admit, the monastery was worth a visit, the sloping vineyards were beautiful. Mind you, we did arrive two hours late at our first overnight stop.

What that holiday made me realise was my tendency to look ahead, to plan all my moves, and to be obsessed with getting there. In that process I failed to see what was around me. I failed to take in the beauty of the journey itself. This is equally true of my spiritual life. I want to 'get there', wherever 'there' is. My prayer is often about the future forgetting that God is with me now. My discipleship is pre-planned, mapped out, each stage sign-posted ahead. Yet who am I following if not the God of the unexpected turn?

Reading the books of Exodus and Numbers we find the story of the pilgrim people of Israel. Led from their slavery in Egypt to the Promised Land of Canaan, they wander about in the desert for forty years. It is precisely this 'wandering' that is important. The journey itself is where Israel encounter their God and where they learn what the Covenant really means. The same is true of pilgrimages to shrines around the world. The arduous task of travelling is all part of the purpose. Even in our own text of John chapter four, it is while Jesus is on the journey that he meets the woman. The destination of Galilee is really only secondary to the story.

So, on our journey: where do we stop for rest? Where do we draw breath? Where do we draw life, recuperate? Jesus, we are told, stops at the well of Jacob which is by a cross-roads. He knows the way ahead and which path to take. What choices face us at this moment? Do we bring them before God in prayer? It strikes me that some people are decision-makers and some are not. I am definitely not. I have stuck to my filing cabinet a magnetic Irish sheep which a close friend sent me some years ago. It reminds me that when it comes to leadership I follow the crowd. One thing I've noticed about agonising over decisions is that I can tend to choose something quite quickly but then mull over it again and again. This was echoed recently in someone who had eventually decided to try his vocation to religious life. He told me that once he had finally plucked up the courage to talk it through with a friend, he'd realised he had made his decision months before. Serious, life-committing decisions are hard – of course they are – and they require prayer; but they require honest prayer. Sitting before the Lord pretending to labour over something which, in our hearts, we have already decided is a little pointless. Sitting before the Lord and saying, "I'm going to do this – but your will be done," is powerful. If we open our hearts to the will of God he will lead us. We may go down a cul-de-sac for a part of our lives but if we are honest in our discernment God will be found – indeed will find us – even down that cul-de-sac.

C. S. Lewis comments, in his story, *The Great Divorce*, that we do not live in a world where

> *...all roads are radii of a circle, and where all, if followed long enough, will therefore draw gradually nearer and finally meet at the centre.*[4]

Rather, he argues, we live in a world where every road forks into two after a couple of miles.

> *I do not think that all those who choose the wrong roads perish, but their rescue consists in being put back on the right road. A wrong sum can be put right: but only by going back till you find the error and working it afresh from that point, never simply by going on.*[5]

I agree that for most of our spiritual lives we sit at a fork or a cross-roads. Every now and then we pluck up the courage and make a move. After not too long we find ourselves at another cross-roads or another fork. The choice of sin or grace is constantly before us. Our consolation is that the way of grace is actually a road to somewhere, whereas very quickly we realise that the way of sin is nothing but a dead end. However, unlike Lewis, I don't believe that we necessarily have to go back. Lewis comments, "evil can be undone, but it cannot develop into good." But can what is evil always be undone? Is the evil of Christ's crucifixion *undone* in the Resurrection or *transfigured*? It seems to me that if, stuck down the dead end lane of sin, we turn again to God he will open up a new possibility, a new direction – if you like, a short cut that will lead us away from the cul-de-sac of sin back to the road of holiness. Surely this is the whole basis of Christian hope? We were dead in our sins but Christ came and opened up a whole new horizon of life. Grace is precisely that rough trail which takes us away from the dead end we got ourselves into, back to a life with direction and future. And this 'short cut' is entirely gratuitous and unexpected. We cannot find our own way back. We cannot move on. We turn to God, desperately lost.

Jesus stops at the well near Sychar, in Samaria; a foreign country. For our own life of discipleship we can often feel in a foreign land. Indeed, St Paul talks about being exiled from the Lord as long as we are at home in the body. Yet he insists that even in this exile, "we are full of confidence, then, and long instead to be exiled from the body and to be at home with the Lord" (2 Cor 5:7-8). This isn't a reference to some sort of material-spiritual divide. Paul's comments need to be seen in the light of his words to the Romans:

In hope, we already have salvation; in hope, not visibly present, or we should not be hoping – nobody goes on hoping for something which he can already see. But having this hope for what we cannot yet see, we are able to wait for it with persevering confidence (Rom 8:24-25).

Our feelings of exile stem from the very hope of our salvation. We yearn for the Promised Land but are all too aware of being in the desert.

We can feel foreigners in other ways too. We can feel isolated, out of sorts, unwanted. Sometimes it may even seem as if other people are speaking in a foreign language. We may be misunderstood. Sadly, this is often the case in our parishes. Being new to the area, being a convert, simply being a little shy can all make us feel out of things. Being single, being divorced, simply being a little different can all make us feel unwanted. It shouldn't be this way, but it is.

Another area of alienation is the area of sin.

There are two distortions of approach to this subject. Firstly, to take it too seriously. Secondly, not to take it seriously enough. As with all things discernment is needed. To know ourselves, warts and all, is to stand before God in prayer. As we grow closer to God we become more aware of our need for his grace. As we move towards God we necessarily move away from sin. Yet if we let sin and guilt take a hold of our lives we can become alienated. If we focus on how we fail we become failures. If we look to God's mercy and love we become his children. Remember the story of the prodigal son in Luke's Gospel. The son returns having failed in his life of debauchery. The Father's response is nothing other than: 'Son of mine' (Lk 15:24).

Equally, we cannot simply dismiss our sins. The current trend to disregard the Sacrament of Reconciliation is wrong. It's not easy to confess our faults. It is even harder is to recognise them in the first place. Unless we bring ourselves before God and say the words of Peter, "Leave me, Lord, I am a sinful man," we will never truly hear the Lord's response: "Do not be afraid, from now on it is people you will be catching" (Lk 5:8-11). If we do not admit our sins we will never be ready to take up our discipleship.

Jesus, then, sits by the well at the cross-roads in a foreign land, tired by his journey. We too can become tired. We lead busy, frantic lives trying to balance all sorts of daily demands and commitments. We have families and work. We have friends. We are trying to make time for prayer and live sincere spiritual lives. We have ministries and parish life. Tiredness sets in that is at the same time physical, mental and emotional. We are not machines. Part of that tiredness can come from our tendency to compartmentalise. We have our work. We have our family. We have our faith. Each makes demands and we play one off against another. The danger here is that God too becomes simply another option, something we fit in between watching the telly and doing the washing up. If we're not careful we begin to practise our faith at pretty much the same level as we 'practise' the piano, or our squash stroke. As a priest, where you would expect 'work' and 'faith' to be more or less integrated, the same tendency occurs. Priests talk of their 'prayer-lives' as if they were something different from their ordinary lives. The balance and rhythm envisaged in St Benedict's Rule shows us a way out of this sort of tiredness: everything can become the *Opus Dei* if only we put nothing above the love of Christ.[6] In other words, God isn't to be seen as an option but as the foundation, context, and goal of all that we do. God is the 'big picture', if you like, in which all the minor brush strokes of life make sense. God is the reality which makes everything else real.

This tendency to compartmentalise God can bring about another sort of tiredness and one which is much more subtle and dangerous than that already described. This is spiritual tiredness: a complacency; an 'I've-seen-it-all-before' approach to life and discipleship. St Benedict, in writing his Rule, talked about *acedia* – a spiritual sloth or laziness. Before him, Cassian and Evagrius had also referred to a spiritual listlessness in their monks.[7] We can become worn down almost with the routine of our lives unless we let God nourish us. A classic example is that of Eucharistic ministry. Remember how honoured and unworthy we felt – yes, and nervous – the first time we administered Holy Communion. Of course with time we grew more confident. Sooner or later, however, familiarity crept in and so did tiredness. We began to take it all for granted. We stopped thinking about what we were really doing.

Another example is prayer. Whether we find the time to give over to meditation each day or to pray the rosary; whether we pray the Divine Office or our own brand of morning and evening prayer, tiredness crops up again and again. We rattle through texts. We fall half asleep. We gradually give less and less time. Giving in to spiritual tiredness can lead to a sort of heavy-heartedness. The Mass, daily prayer, examination of conscience – these can all become a real chore. We can find ourselves reluctantly, perhaps even resentfully, going through the motions. In the end some of us give up all together.

Acedia leads us into compromise: a bit of petty pilfering at work, fiddling our car expenses, short-changing people, ignoring those we find difficult, indulging time and again in sexual fantasy, becoming increasing prone to road rage, or other angry outbursts. They may be small examples, but nevertheless they are compromises; symptoms perhaps of a deeper malaise. When we stop noticing and when we start justifying – it is then that we have at some level surrendered, not to God, but to our own selfishness.

Complacency, spiritual tiredness, *acedia* – these are the enemies of discipleship. Being a disciple of Christ means serving others. Ministry is service. Complacency is me. Tiredness raises the questions: How do *I* feel? How am *I* today? How confident am *I* in this situation? How used to it all am *I*? *Me*? Ministry, discipleship is not about me – it's about Christ. Listen to the Baptist's response to his murmuring followers: "He must grow greater, I must grow less" (Jn 3:30).

How, then, do we cope with such tiredness? Practical tiredness demands practical responses. It demands that we are sensible, that we make priorities and stick to them, that we learn to say 'no' at times. Spiritual tiredness is harder. It seems to me that we can learn from the lives of the saints. People like St Benedict. People like St Thérèse of Lisieux. We can come to share their vision of the Kingdom of God. Like them, we can allow that Kingdom to take hold of our lives. This means recognising our tendency to compartmentalise; realising when we make God just yet another option. It also means being like the lepers, and the demoniacs, and the haemorrhaging woman of the gospels: believing that in our very tiredness and in our very need we can encounter the Christ.

Encountering Christ

When a Samaritan woman came to draw water, Jesus said to her, "Give me something to drink." His disciples had gone into the town to buy food. The Samaritan woman said to him, "You are a Jew. How is it that you ask me, a Samaritan, for something to drink?" – Jews, of course, do not associate with Samaritans (Jn 4:7-9).

It always makes me smile to imagine the nonchalant way in which the Evangelist says, "Jews, of course, do not associate with Samaritans." I picture the Beloved Disciple retelling this story in the early Johannine community with an air of Oscar Wilde about him. I see his listeners vigorously nodding their heads and murmuring their assent. For ourselves too the rivalry of Jew and Samaritan is rather old hat; or is it?

The origins of such rivalry lay deeply embedded in the ancient history of the two groups. We know that until the reigns of David and Solomon there existed a loose relationship between the different tribes of Israel. According to Scripture it was David who, having reigned in Judah for seven years, captured Jerusalem and managed to unify the country. After the death of Solomon, in 931 BC, Israel divided into two kingdoms. The northern kingdom of Israel had Samaria as its capital. The southern kingdom of Judah had Jerusalem and the Temple. We can follow the gradual decline of the two kingdoms in the historical writings of the Old Testament. What we find is the slow, cancerous growth of mutual suspicion and distrust. In 721 BC Samaria fell to the Assyrian Empire and the northern kingdom became a weak vassal state. Judah, however, held out until 598 BC. Then the Babylonian Empire sacked Jerusalem and destroyed the Temple.

During this long period there was political and religious intrigue aplenty. The north came to be despised by the Jews for their intermixing with foreigners and foreign gods. By the time of the Edict of Cyrus I in 538 BC, which allowed the exiled Jews to re-inhabit Jerusalem, the suspicion had all but cemented. Although the region of Samaria contained many of the ancient shrines of Judaism, the Samaritans became despised as polluted and adulterous. When the Jewish community began to rebuild the Temple the Samaritans had hoped to assist, but were rejected outright. So they then bedevilled the construction and caused delay. They went on to oppose the building of the walls of Jerusalem and the hatred between the two groups became sealed.

By Jesus' time, the opposition of Jew and Samaritan was well attested and was based on historical, religious, and ethnic grounds. To the Jew, the Samaritans had become a diluted perversion of what true Judaism was all about. Historically, they had hindered the Jewish return to their Promised Land. Religiously, they ignored the Temple and focused instead on shrines such as Bethel (where Jacob had his dream in Genesis 28:10-22). Ethnically, they had permitted intermarriage with other races and cultures and were no longer fit to be a part of the Chosen Race. They were to be avoided at all costs.

We can assume that everything in Jesus' socio-historical conditioning, religious upbringing, and understanding of Jewish history should have prevented him from even acknowledging this woman who comes to the well. There were most likely ritual taboos on Jews using the same drinking and eating utensils as Samaritans. Nine hundred years of history says, "Ignore this woman." Yet Jesus says, "Give me something to drink."

How can we imagine the situation of Jesus and the Samaritan woman in today's terms? It's like Ian Paisley buying Gerry Adams a pint. It's like a survivor of the Holocaust defending Adolf Hitler. It just will not happen. But it does. Why? Because Jesus is thirsty. To my mind it is as simple as that. History, religious hatred, ethnic differences, all give way to one of the most basic human needs: thirst. If you were a betting person at the time of Christ never, at any odds, would you place a bet on this: Jesus will ask a Samaritan woman for a drink – and yet that is what he does. This encounter with the Christ comes about because the Son of God has become human and is thirsty.

Where, then, do we encounter the Christ? Precisely in our humanity. Precisely in our human weakness and our need. Isn't this one of the central themes of St Paul?

He has answered me, "My grace is enough for you: for power is at full stretch in weakness." It is, then, about my weakness that I am happiest of all to boast, so that the power of Christ may rest upon me; and that is why I am glad of weaknesses, insults, constraints, persecutions and distress for Christ's sake. For it is when I am weak that I am strong (2 Cor 12:9-10).

So many of the Psalms use terms of human need to speak about encountering God: "God, you are my God, I pine for you; my heart thirsts for you" (Ps 63); "I am exhausted with calling out, my throat is hoarse, my eyes are worn out with searching for my God" (Ps 69); "In the day of my distress I call upon you, because you answer me, Lord" (Ps 86).

The Synoptic gospels show time and again how Jesus responds to the basic needs of others. A favourite example of mine is in Mark 1:40-45. Jesus has begun his Galilean ministry. Having spent some time in Capernaum teaching and healing, he is on the move again. A leper falls to his knees before the Lord and pleads with him saying, "If you are willing, you can cleanse me." Now most translations say something along the lines of, "Feeling sorry for him, Jesus stretched out his hand, touched him, said to him, 'I am willing. Be cleansed.' And at once the skin-disease left him and he was cleansed." However, some early manuscripts say, "Filled with anger, Jesus stretched out his hand and touched him."

To understand the implications of this fully we need to remind ourselves of what leprosy implied in biblical times. Almost all disfiguring skin diseases were lumped together as leprosy. None of them had a rabbinical cure. They were accepted as a divine punishment for some sin or other. Lepers were outcasts, abandoned by God, untouchable. So, in Mark's account, we have the human need of a man cast out from society, ill and desperate. He comes to Jesus, who is filled with anger at this situation. Jesus' instinctive reaction is to touch the untouchable: to reach out and break taboos because someone is in need.

The situation of the woman at the well seems different though. Surely here it is not Jesus responding to someone else's need but Jesus acting from his own need. In fact the irony of the situation comes out in the following discussion. It is revealed that the Samaritan has a far more basic human need than Jesus' thirst. She needs to be loved by God. Ultimately it is this which allows Jesus to break through the taboo, to break down nine hundred years of hatred and suspicion.

What, then, is our approach to human need? How do we view weakness? What sort of Christianity do we practise? There is a difference, I think, between a robust Christianity and an 'action man' Christianity. We are most certainly called to be robust: to have no dread or fear, but simply to proclaim the Lord; to stand firm against the devil.[8] And yet, there is the temptation to become the all action hero. It is a temptation I succumb to myself in priestly ministry. A tendency to reject my own weakness and believe that I, and I alone, can save others from theirs. The danger of thinking that everything depends upon me. *Our* ministry, *our* gifts, *our* time, *our* resources. When that notion is shown up for the vanity that it is, sadly it can be the occasion for our spiritual tiredness to assert itself once again.

A recent vocations promotional video was reviewed by *The Times* which complimented it as portraying priesthood as an exciting and demanding career. I wonder whether this type of promotion doesn't fall into the 'action man' category. The preaching of the apostles doesn't speak of exciting careers. The writings of the New Testament tell of weak men and women being the earthenware vessels holding the treasure and immensity of God's power and design (2 Cor 4:7). Something that bespeaks career, excitement, 'action man' must be misguided. The call to priesthood, just like the call to religious life or the call to marriage, comes from the basic baptismal call to holiness. Holiness is not to be found in a career structure, or an exciting game plan. Holiness is to be found here and now, in my human weakness, whenever I let God love me.

An 'action man' Christianity has no time for weakness. It looks to heroes and heroines. It expects valour at all times. It sees in the Cross the fearless stoicism of the Redeemer and fails to hear the anguished cry: "*Eloi, Eloi, lama sabachthani?*" (Mk 15:34). An 'action man' Christianity doesn't boast with St Paul of his weaknesses but talks of victories won and wars waged. This sort of able-bodied, hale and hearty discipleship forms the basis for the worst forms of hypocrisy. Sins smothered, hidden, but never forgiven. Weaknesses denied, closeted, but lurking nevertheless.

On the other hand, there are dangers with over stressing weakness. St Paul is quite clear in his letter to the Romans, when he says,

Should we remain in sin so that grace may be given the more fully? Out of the question! We have died to sin; how can we go on living in it? (Rom 6:1-2).

Just because we are not called to be 'action man' Christians, it doesn't imply that we have to be wimps. One of the great dangers of meditative prayer is that we can end up meditating upon ourselves; navel-gazingly cosseting ourselves in our own infirmities.

We encounter Christ in our need, which includes our weakness and our sin. The whole purpose of the parable of the Pharisee and the Publican in Luke 18:9-14 is that the tax-collector cannot pray like the Pharisee. In his muted desperation, he cries out from the heart: "God, be merciful to me, a sinner." And Jesus' pronouncement is absolute: "This man, I tell you, went home again justified."

The message in Jesus asking the Samaritan woman for a drink is this: there can be no barrier, no taboo, no excuse – be it religious, ethnic, social, historical, or whatever – which can separate us from meeting Christ in human need. So when we are confronted with spiritual tiredness, it is precisely then that we can find the Lord. Let our very tiredness – like Jesus' thirst, like the woman's deeper need for love – let our situation cry out to the Redeemer.

Irresistible love

If you only knew what God is offering and who it is that is saying to you, "Give me something to drink," you would have been the one to ask, and he would have given you living water (Jn 4:10).

An abiding image of my childhood stems from when I was four. I had done something naughty – I can't remember now what it was – and had been caught out. I was terrified of what my parents would do and so I ran and hid underneath this enormous dining-room table that we had at the time. Whereas my reaction was to flee, my mother's was to come looking for me. I recall my heart almost stopping as I saw from beneath the table my mother's legs standing in front of me. I knew that this was it: I had to face the music. In fact what happened was that my mum bent down, scooped me out from my hiding place, and hugged me. I was crying, and she was soothing me. I was awaiting my terrible scolding, and all I received was unconditional love.

Isn't this the stuff of redemption? St John records Jesus telling Nicodemus, "For God sent his Son into the world not to judge the world, but so that through him the world might be saved" (Jn 3:17). Our hope in God is not to be based upon fear of punishment and earning the heavenly banquet by our good deeds, but on the certainty of being loved by God.

St Thérèse tells of this certainty in her parable of the fledgling bird[9] gazing up at the sun. Around the sun majestic eagles soar high into the sky. The eagles represent the great saints and the sun represents God. The little bird is Thérèse herself. She may not be able to fly towards the sun and encircle it like the saints, but she fixes her gaze and flaps her wings to show where her heart lies. A storm brews, clouds cover the sun, and the wind and the rain assault the tiny chick. Not for one moment does she avert her gaze. Even though she is wet through and can no longer see the sun or feel the warmth of its presence, she remains fixed, staring ever heavenward. Thérèse's own life displayed precisely this certainty of being loved. She died aged twenty-four of tuberculosis having suffered not only physically but also having endured a total blackness and dry state of prayer. But she always fixed her gaze on God and, even when she could not 'feel' his loving presence, she was certain that he loved her.

Let us listen to her own story of a soul:

If, one day in heaven, I find out that You love them more than me, I shall rejoice, recognising that even on earth they must have deserved it more, but meanwhile I cannot imagine any greater love than that You have given me without any merit of my own.[10]

For Thérèse, there could be no doubt that God loved her so much and that she had done nothing to earn it. Even if she discovered that God loved others more than herself, and that in fact they did have some merit, she would be content with the love that she knew.

Julian of Norwich also offers us a parable of such

divine love. In her *Showings* she sees 'a little thing, the size of a hazelnut' and realises that this stands for all that is made. The totality of creation, the heavens and earth, all the universe is shown as tiny and insignificant.

> *I marvelled that it continued to exist and did not suddenly disintegrate; it was so small. And again my mind supplied the answer, "It exists, both now and forever, because God loves it." In short, everything owes its existence to the love of God.*[11]

We know that God's love is the reason for creation. We are sure that God's love is the motive for our redemption. We profess that God's love is gratuitous and without limit. But do we live our lives as people who are so radically loved? I don't. I puff myself up and try to make myself adorable to others and to God. I want God to love me. I want him to notice me. And so I sin like a spoilt child trying to grab attention.

"If you only knew what God is offering," says Jesus to the Samaritan woman. This line is addressed to us too. If we could only begin to understand just what God offers us, our lives would be transformed. We would, like St Thérèse, be able to speak with authority about the things of love. We would, like Mother Julian, use the vivid imagery of being clothed, enfolded, and embraced by God.[12] We would give up sin. We would abandon trying to be loveable and we would let ourselves be lost in God's irresistible love.

I often wonder about Purgatory and what it must be like. A purifying growth of perfection in all our human dimensions is the kind of way most theologians present it today.[13] A process of being made ready to be loved face to face. My thoughts focus on that divine encounter. After our deaths, when we can no longer deny God's love for us, how can we refuse to be perfected? The image I have is of being asked by the Lord to strip down to my bare nakedness. To trust him and to be unabashed by my own inadequacy and insecurity. To let go of those things in which I have wrapped myself during my life – vanity, ambition, conceit, and so on. For the first time to stop playing a part and to admit, this is me, naked, as I am. The pain of that process must be a joyous pain. It must be the pain of slowly realising what a fool I've been; of realising I have been loved all along, without deserving it. I wonder if even the worst sinner, the most evil and conceited genius, can't help themselves but be gently persuaded to let themselves be loved. To let go of self-love before the One who is Irresistible Love. Surely God's love is greater than the greatest sin?

Hell for me remains the condition of the possibility of our free will. At any moment we have the option to reject once and for all the love that God offers. And rejection of that love would indeed be hell. But I cannot conceive of anyone failing to be persuaded to respond to the love of God, when finally they meet him face to face. Is Purgatory, then, a sort of Divine Persuasion?

If only we knew what God is offering us. We do know. It stands out full clear on every page of Scripture. It is never more evident than in the Passion and Resurrection of Christ. And yet we turn elsewhere – we seek a substitute love.

Substitutes

"You have no bucket, sir," she answered, "and the well is deep: how do you get this living water? Are you a greater man than our father Jacob, who gave us this well and drank from it himself with his sons and his cattle?" Jesus replied:

"Whoever drinks this water will be thirsty again; but no one who drinks the water that I shall give him will ever be thirsty again: the water that I shall give him will become in him a spring of water, welling up for eternal life."

"Sir," said the woman, "give me some of that water, so that I may never be thirsty or come here again to draw water" (Jn 4:11-15).

What are the substitutes with which we tend to cram our lives? Possessions, self-importance, pride? People to be seen with, places to go? How much time and energy do we expend on being the right sort of people, who do the right sort of things? It sometimes seems we can never win. Either we get accused of surrounding ourselves with people who make us look intelligent and glamorous, because they are not; or else we are called groupies of those more intelligent and glamorous than ourselves. We look down our noses at those we feel beneath us, but we can be sure that somewhere someone is looking down their nose at us. We clutter our lives with possessions and achievements trying to make something of ourselves. Yet we are critical when we see others doing exactly the same thing.

We even seek spiritual substitutes. Aren't I holy? Aren't others impressed by *my* wisdom and knowledge? Look at the spiritual heights to which *I* can attain. Look at how long *I* pray each day. Listen to *me* and find God. What vanity! The words of St Benedict are apt:

Do not aspire to be called holy before you really are, but first be holy that you may more truly be called so.[14]

One of the greatest temptations to any one seeking holiness of life is that they begin to believe they have found it before they actually have. In the seminary as a deacon or priest we were always encouraged to be good examples to the other students. Fine, but to my mind we should have put our energies not into being good examples, but into our relationship with God: then the example would follow. It is the same in the parish. Do I make sure I'm seen praying to encourage others to pray, or do I just get on with it and be prayerful? Only if my prayer is genuine and not self-seeking will I become an example to those around me.

At the heart of all these substitutes is self-love. Isn't this the fundamental sin attributed to Adam in Genesis? The serpent tempts Eve with the forbidden fruit, saying: "The day you eat it your eyes will be opened and you will be like gods" (Gen 3:5). To be gods with a small 'g'; to be locked up in a self-sufficient self-love – we weren't created for this. We were created to be loved and to love in return. We were created in the image of the Triune God, whose own inner life is the eternal dynamic of illimitable love, loving, and being loved. The result of this first sin is a turning in on ourselves. When God comes to Adam, he no longer rejoices that he communes freely with the Creator but worries about his own nakedness, his own image.

Our substitutes, then, are like clothes in which we dress up for different occasions. We are afraid to be ourselves and so we lie about who we are. We are frightened of rejection and so we search for things to make us acceptable. We try to find meaning to our lives, but the only meaning we can ever have will be found in relation to our Creator.

The Samaritan woman begins to respond to Jesus' offer of living water by making all sorts of excuses: *You have no bucket, the well is deep, surely you're not greater than our father Jacob?* What are our excuses for clinging to our love-substitutes? Why do I have to have *this* car, when a smaller, more economical one will do? Why do I want people to call me by *this title*, when my name is simply this? Why do I waste so much time doing one thing, when something else is more important? Why do I claim to be too busy to pray some days, and then spend the evenings watching television?

I constantly tease a priest friend of mine, who has just had his presbytery redecorated, that he has become like Cardinal Wolsey. In fact the house did need doing up and it is a rich parish with no financial worries. But upholstered pelmets? Hand made tiles around the fireplace? Specially chosen water colours in gilt frames? "What's wrong with wanting beautiful things?" is his stock reply. I'll tell him what's wrong: my jealousy. The self-love and substitute-love in the teasing isn't the rights or wrongs of his interior decor, but my need for 'beautiful things', my need for status. The fact that I dress up my jealousy in critical pseudo-simplicity doesn't change it. An asceticism based upon judgements of those around us is nothing other than a manifestation of pride. It is an echo of the Pharisee, "I thank you God that I am not grasping, unjust, adulterous like everyone else" (Lk 18:11). There is little point trying to strip ourselves of the substitutes we find for God, if we then go on to focus on the perceived substitutes of others. The purpose of any genuine ascetic practice is to allow us to look upon God without distraction.

Jesus says, "Whoever drinks this water will be thirsty again; but no one who drinks the water that I shall give him will ever be thirsty again." Our substitutes, whatever they be, can never satisfy us like the real thing: the love of God. A pious image that I rather like is the one of the Beloved Disciple leaning on Christ's breast at the Last Supper, drinking in his words and presence. Origen says of John's Gospel:

Only he can understand this Gospel who has laid his head on Jesus' breast and taken Mary as his mother.[15]

As disciples we are called to lean upon the breast of the Saviour we follow and to drink deeply from him. In other words to waste time in his company, to take in and imbibe his words, his truth, his attitudes, his vision; to grow like him in every way. Only in his presence will we find the courage to let go of our substitutes. Only by finding time to be with him in prayer will we begin to believe that he loves us.

What if I don't thirst for God? What if my tiredness has taken over such that I am barren and dry and no amount of prayer will change this? What if I have lost even the want to pray and to be with Christ? St Ignatius Loyola urges us: if we don't pray or even have the desire to pray, then start by praying for the desire to pray. J. M. Crum's words, quoted at the beginning of this chapter, are apt here:

Fields of our heart that dead and bare have been:
Love is come again like wheat that springeth green.

The resurrection promises us the hope of new life, new energy, new love, even in the dry and dusty tiredness of death; but we must co-operate. It is up to us to begin to open our hearts to the Love on offer. We, as Ignatius urges us, must pray even from our barren desperation.

Jesus goes on, "The water that I shall give him will become in him a spring of water, welling up for eternal life." This always reminds me of a televised Mass I watched years ago. The parish seemed to take 'meaningfulness' to its limits in the liturgy. The response to the Bidding prayers was: "Water from the side of Christ, well up within us." At the time I thought it was hilarious, because it sounded so strange but everyone said it so straight-faced. And yet I remember it. In fact it captured something important about our prayer. Our relationship with Christ is essentially dynamic. Water welling up is water on the move. The very notion of 'welling up' creates in my mind the picture of overflowing, or of bursting out. The love which God offers us is precisely this ecstatic, dynamic stuff. Ecstatic is a good word because it literally means *out of being*, a gratuitous love which is from the essence of God, and therefore cannot be contained.

Whatever substitutes we choose in life, they will never be able to supplant our need for God. Our lives of discipleship are lives to be lived in love – dynamic, moving, growing, changing. The love of God *must* change us. It leads us on and away from sin and substitutes and self-love, and into God himself.

Sin

"Go and call your husband," said Jesus to her, "and come back here." The woman answered, "I have no husband." Jesus said to her, "You are right to say "I have no husband"; for although you have had five, the one you now have is not your husband. You spoke the truth there" (Jn 4:16-19).

"The Catholic Church is obsessed with sin." This is the conclusion of a close friend of mine. "Just look at all the prayers," she goes on, "Save us from this, forgive us that. Sin here. Sin there." Of course the Church is concerned with sin. Sin is a part of the reality of our lives and the Church tries to make sense of that reality. Any creed that doesn't attempt to deal with sin seems to me to be lacking somewhat. But there is another reason for our obsession with sin. It is from sin that we are redeemed. As the Easter Proclamation says, "O happy fault. O necessary sin of Adam which won for us so great a redeemer." Sin and redemption go hand in hand.

"Go and call your husband." In the story, Jesus changes the whole topic of conversation and so wrong-foots the Samaritan woman. She inadvertently blurts out the truth about her personal life. I see the scene as rather comic. Jesus, seeming to know the details of her life, tricks her into admitting the messiness of her living arrangements: "I have no husband." It now becomes even more evident that it is not Jesus who is tired and in need, but the Samaritan herself. A tired, sinful woman in need of redemption. A woman who has certainly lived, having had five husbands and currently living with someone not her husband. Jesus' reaction to the truth about the woman is not condemnation, but almost a knowing laugh: "You spoke the truth there."

I think there is something important here. We do take sin seriously, as Christians, but we mustn't take it too seriously. Becoming guilt-stricken, fearful, screwed up sinners is not what redemption is all about. A sense of humour, a sense of relief that salvation means forgiveness and a new future is what comes out of the Samaritan woman's encounter with Christ. Jesus leads her on and away from sin to a recognition that he is the Messiah. It is similar to the scene of the adulterous woman:

> *Jesus again straightened up and said, "Woman, where are they? Has no one condemned you?" "No one, sir," she replied. "Neither do I condemn you," said Jesus. "Go away, and from this moment sin no more"* (Jn 8:10-11).

Surely what will echo in the adulterous woman's mind are those final words: "From this moment sin no more." Imagine her relief. She is free, not only from the certain death by stoning that she faced, but from sin. She now has a future. Listen to the words of St Paul:

Christ set us free, so that we should remain free. Stand firm, then, and do not let yourselves be fastened again to the yoke of slavery (Gal 5:1).

How difficult it is to laugh at ourselves. Perhaps it is because deep down we don't really like what we find. One of the most startling penances I have ever received in Confession was to be told: "Go out and enjoy yourself." It was precisely what I needed: to let go of my sins, and all the bits of me that I don't particularly like, and to enjoy redemption.

Julian of Norwich has an image of Christ inviting his friends to a banquet and suffusing the whole occasion with 'joy and cheer'.[16] Julian also talks of laughing heartily when she saw that Christ had overcome the devil.[17] What comes across clearly in the fourteenth century mystic is the confidence of God's power to save. Sin has nothing to offer; evil cannot defend itself against the onslaught of Christ's passion, and so we can laugh in its face. Redemption is something to be enjoyed.

Rather than rejoice in God's loving forgiveness, we tend to hide our sins from ourselves and from God. Even those who make frequent use of the Sacrament of Reconciliation can subconsciously bury those things of which they are most ashamed. We try to forget what's lurking in our closet. If we are committed in prayer, sooner or later the truth slips out. Sooner or later we learn that God loves us as we are, even in our sin. Again let us listen to the words of St Paul:

You could hardly find anyone ready to die even for someone upright; though it is just possible that, for a really good person, someone might undertake to die. So it is proof of God's own love for us, that Christ died for us while we were still sinners (Rom 5:7-8).

The moments when God pokes fun at us, and at our silly, sinful lives are precious moments. It is then as if he says to us, "At last, you're being yourself. At last, you're letting me love you." How much time do we waste being bogged down in our failure, or screwed up by our sins? Pray, and let the truth slip out. Let God laugh at us.

Revelation

The woman said to him, "I know that Messiah – that is, Christ – is coming; and when he comes he will explain everything." Jesus said, "That is who I am, I who speak to you" (Jn 4:25-26).

Just before these lines in the text, Jesus has spoken to the Samaritan woman about the true place of worship. He advises her, "God is spirit, and those who worship must worship in spirit and in truth" (Jn 4:24). In other words, the time has now come when places of worship are unimportant. What is now important is whether or not I chose to worship with all my life-force and being; whether I chose to worship in total integrity, or whether I prefer to continue with my current half-measures and tired compromises. All of this is leading up to the question, *so are you the Messiah, then?*

It is mind-blowing that Jesus should reveal his true identity to a Samaritan woman, after a chance encounter at a well. Scripture scholars point to the significance of the well. The Essenes described the *Torah* as being like a well dug by their teachers from which they drew knowledge of the truth.[18] In this text of John, Jesus replaces the *Torah* as the source of truth and salvation. He, now, is the well from which to draw. It is in Christ that we can worship in spirit and in truth.

So the Samaritan hesitantly raises the question of the Messiah: "He will explain everything." Jesus replies, "That is who I am." We know of course that this statement is more than simply, *I am a Messiah*. Jesus uses the divine name, *Yahweh*. It is Jesus himself who offers the woman a new life, as the fountain of God's forgiveness and love.

This encounter arises from the ordinary and everyday; from a tired, weary, thirsty journey. The implications for ourselves are obvious: the love that is being revealed in Christ Jesus is a gift offered and to be accepted in the everyday moments. We don't need to look for signs. We need simply to accept what Jesus offers us here and now.

NOTES

1. Cf. Jn 1:38 in the Revised Standard Version.
2. Cf. Jn 2:1-25; 3:22-36.
3. J. Sobrino, (trans. P. Burns and F. McDonagh), *Jesus the Liberator. A Historical-Theological Reading of Jesus of Nazareth*, Burns & Oates, 1994, p. 267.
4. C. S. Lewis, *The Great Divorce*. (Fount Paperbacks), HarperCollins Publishers Ltd., 1946, p. 7.
5. *Ibid.*, pp. 7-8.
6. *Rule of St Benedict* IV, 21.
7. Cf. G. Holzherr, (trans. Glenstal Abbey) *The Rule of Benedict. A Guide to Christian Living*, Four Courts Press Ltd., Dublin, 1994, p. 223.
8. Cf. 1 Peter 3:13-15; 5:8-9.
9. *Collected letters of St Thérèse of Lisieux*, edited by the Abbe Combes, (trans. F. Sheed), Sheed & Ward, London, 1949, 248-251. See also J. Udris, *Holy Daring. The Fearless Trust of St Thérèse of Lisieux*, Gracewing, 1997, pp. 62-76.
10. *The Autobiography of St Thérèse of Lisieux. The Story of a Soul*, translated by J. Beevers, Doubleday, 1989, p. 147.

11. Julian of Norwich, (trans. C. Wolters), *Revelations of Divine Love*, (Penguin Classics), p. 68.
12. *Ibid* pp. 67-68.
13. Cf. K. Rahner & H. Vorgrimler, *Concise Theological Dictionary*, London, 2nd ed., 1983, pp. 426-427.
14. Rule of St Benedict, IV, 62.
15. Cf. Origen's Commentary on John 1:4.
16. Julian of Norwich, *Revelations of Divine Love*, chapter 14.
17. *Ibid.*, chapter 13.
18. See *Jerome Biblical Commentary* for John 4:23-24. See also J. McPolin, *John*, Veritas, 1979, pp. 78-79.

2
The Way of Love

Reflections on the Washing of the Feet
John 13:1-15

*Love is the way.
If you want to believe – then love;
if you want to understand your faith – then love;
if you want to discover the secrets
of Christ's truth – then love is still the way.*

(William of St Thierry)

The sign we give

Before the festival of the Passover, Jesus, knowing that his hour had come to pass from this world to the Father, having loved those who were his in the world, loved them to the end.

They were at supper, and the devil had already put it into the mind of Judas Iscariot son of Simon to betray him (Jn 13:1-2).

In 1995 the Bishops of England and Wales produced a document on collaborative ministry entitled, *The Sign We Give*. In it they presented a number of models of such ministry. To my mind the most important definition proffered was the following:

Collaborative ministry begins from a fundamental desire to work together because we are called by the Lord to be a company of disciples, not isolated individuals[1]

The call to discipleship is also a call to community. Throughout the gospels we have all sorts of examples of the disciples being and working together. Perhaps the most poignant, though, is the account of the Last Supper in John. Here, on the eve of Christ's passion, on the very night the disciples will scatter, Jesus presents to them the most profound sign yet: the Eucharist. However, in John's account there is no institution narrative. There is no, "This is my body, this is the cup of my blood." There is simply the washing of feet.

Theologians and Scripture scholars find varying reasons for this. Some argue that the Johannine tradition, which produced the Fourth Gospel, opted to draw on the early Christian association of the Eucharist with the miracle of the manna in the Old Testament, and so had already provided the reader with a Eucharistic exposition in chapter six. Others take John's account alongside the Synoptic tradition and believe that John is presenting us with the practical, concrete implications of what the Eucharist is: the expression of God's love for us. The Eucharist is God's gift to his Church as a sign of his love. The washing of feet is that selfsame love expressed in a different way. God loves us so much that he comes among us as one who serves. When we receive the Eucharist we let God wash our feet.

The Eucharist is, then, something profoundly humbling. We often focus on our own unworthiness to receive the Lord in this great sacrament. There is a danger in this: if we focus on ourselves, we fail to perceive what God is doing. If we overly worry about *our* unworthiness, we miss the tremendous love of God who gently serves and generously nourishes us.

The Last Supper brings the apostles together in a new way. There is an awareness of something significant about to happen. They are on the eve of that terrible ordeal of love, Christ's Passion. They are given a sign and are called to give that sign to others. In the Church, we celebrate the Eucharist daily and are daily called to live out the washing of feet. The sign that God gives is clear: unconditional love. But what of the sign that we give, as the modern day community of disciples?

The scene begins with St John heightening the tension. The festival of the Passover is near. It is the eve of Jesus' passion and death. The devil had put it into the mind of Judas to betray him. John uses the expression, the 'hour'. We find it at the wedding feast at Cana where Jesus replies to his mother's intervention about the lack of wine, "My hour has not come yet" (Jn 2:4). We find it used in the discussion with the Samaritan woman when Jesus says, "The hour is coming, indeed is already here, when true worshippers will worship the Father in spirit and truth" (Jn 4:23). Again, John quotes Jesus as saying, "The hour is coming when the dead will leave their graves" (Jn 5:28), and "What shall I say: Father, save me from this hour? But it is for this very reason that I have come to this hour. Father, glorify your name" (Jn 12:27-28). At other points John explains why Jesus isn't arrested sooner: "Because his hour had not yet come no one laid a hand on him" (Jn 7:30; 8:20).

The 'hour' in John is Jesus' death on a cross. The crucifixion is the moment when his mission is accomplished. He returns to the Father having completed his revelation of love. Everything in the Gospel has been leading up to this event. The cross is *the sign* of God's loving presence.

We can imagine the tension for Jesus and his followers. John has already told us in chapter eleven that expectations were running high in Jerusalem:

> *Many of the country people who had gone up to Jerusalem before the Passover to purify themselves were looking out for Jesus, saying to one another as they stood about in the Temple, "What do you think? Will he come to the festival or not?"* (Jn 11:55-56).

In the following chapter, Jesus rides triumphantly into the city on a donkey, being proclaimed Messiah. The Romans are jittery – will there be a riot? The religious leaders are concerned that he will incite the crowds, or perhaps be used by the Zealots to start mob protests and violence. The whole fragile politico-religious deal which allows them to keep their Temple worship looks threatened. Even the Twelve must have been affected by this tension. What will the Master do next? Will they all be arrested? What of the crowds? Will someone betray him?

In the midst of this Jesus gives his followers the sign of humble service and love, and commands them to do likewise. It is almost as if the Love of God has closed its eyes to the hostile threat of human rejection in its determination to continue loving. It's as if God in Christ was saying to the world, "Do your worst to me. I for my part will show you how to love and be loved."

Humility

Jesus knew that the Father had put everything into his hands, and that he had come from God and was returning to God, and he got up from table, removed his outer garments and, taking a towel, wrapped it round his waist; he then poured water into a basin and began to wash his disciples' feet and to wipe them with the towel he was wearing (Jn 13:2-5).

In one of her books, Sheila Cassidy, a major force behind the hospice movement in this country, talks about how as a doctor she sometimes hides behind her white coat and stethoscope; how she sometimes retreats into professionalism as a way of coping with her terminally ill patients. She is making a good point and one that resonates with me as a priest. How often do I hide behind my dog collar because I can't handle a situation. How often do I rely on preconceptions others have of priests to avoid being myself?

We do tend to conceal our true and insecure natures by playing certain parts. It even happens in marriages, when honesty between a couple breaks down and they revert to particular roles. One of the problems with giving people nicknames, however affectionate, is that the person starts to live out the character. The name begins to define and limit them. It is indicative of the insight of the Ancient

Near East that there was a strong belief in the power of names. To know someone's name meant to have control over them. We see this idea in the Scriptures with the increasing avoidance of using the name, Yahweh. No one can have power over God and so no one must say his name. Yet the very revelation of the divine name is itself illimitable. Most translations render God's words from the burning bush to Moses as, "I am who I am."[2] The way Hebrew works, this could also be translated in English as, "I was who I was" and "I will be who I will be." In other words, "I define myself."

We sinners attempt to define ourselves by the construction of roles to play, of images to project. In reality we can only be defined in relation to our God, for our essential definition is given in Genesis:

> *God created man in the image of himself, in the image of God he created him, male and female he created them* (Gen 1:27).

Our true identity and role in life becomes clearer the more we respond to God's call. Isn't this what the Church means when she talks about different vocations? The Latin verb, *vocare* means to call. It can also mean to summon, to invite, to name, and to designate. We are, all of us, summoned, or invited, by God to be other than the sinners that we are. We are, all of us, designated for holiness and named his chosen ones. To take up that divine invitation means abandoning our self-projected images and allowing God to be the image that shines through us. St Paul put it succinctly:

And all of us, with our unveiled faces like mirrors reflecting the glory of the Lord, are being transformed into the image that we reflect in brighter and brighter glory; this is the working of the Lord who is the Spirit (2 Cor 3:18).

Thomas Merton, in his autobiography, *The Seven Story Mountain*, told of how he began his journey into priesthood by believing himself called to be a Franciscan. In the months before his proposed entry into the noviciate, he realised that his meditative prayer had become largely a day-dream. He would imagine himself wearing the brown robe and white cord of a friar, walking about in sandals with a shaved head.[3] He was still too tied up with self-image to hear where God was really calling him. It is ironic that someone feeling called to follow St Francis, who stood naked before the bishop of Assisi, should concern himself with what clothes he would wear. No wonder, then, that Merton's vocation actually lay elsewhere.

Jesus, we hear, strips down, removing his outer garments. This is a practical preparation for what he is about to do: wash the disciples' feet; but it brings to mind the next occasion we will hear of him being stripped. Jesus as he is crucified is stripped of his clothes and the soldiers even cast lots for his seamless inner garment.[4]

Jesus, then, shows us a God who is prepared to strip down for love of us. Clothing can represent wealth and status. We dress up to go out to posh restaurants. We wear certain clothes at work. We make an effort at baptisms and weddings and funerals. What we wear says something. We judge others by their clothing: rich and poor; tasteful or common; young or old; fashionable or not. Clothing can also represent protection, security, survival, and warmth. Think of hard hats and steel cap boots. Think of army camouflage and policemen's tunics. Think of woolly hats and fake fur coats. Nakedness, on the other hand, tells of intimacy and vulnerability. It is significant that it is with Adam's sin that nakedness becomes a thing to be covered up. Jesus shows us a love that reverses this and removes barriers, security, and status. Jesus shows us an intimate love.

How do we imagine the scene of Jesus washing his disciples' feet? Their feet would have been hot, sweaty and dusty from their travelling and the usual hospitality consisted of providing water for each of the guests to wash their own feet. But here Jesus takes on the task himself, as a sign of loving service. It always reminds me of shoe-shiners. A few years ago there would often be boy-scouts at Norwich train station offering to shine travellers' shoes. They would crouch down before their customers and get on with their polishing. It struck me that you couldn't even see their faces. Is this the humble love of God, who crouches and abases himself before his own creatures?

An image I prefer is of a parent washing and drying the tiny feet of their little child. The gentle massaging and towelling. The love and care that is being expressed. The constant glances between mother and child or father and child, giving reassurance. Surely this is the humble love of God?

God as loving Father, loving Mother, taking care of our tiny feet, reassuring us, being gentle.

Humility, then, is not something debasing. Jesus isn't grovelling before his disciples. He is displaying genuine warmth and love, casting aside rank and dignity in order to care for them.

Understanding

He came to Simon Peter, who said to him, "Lord, are you going to wash my feet?" Jesus answered, "At the moment you do not know what I am doing, but later you will understand."

"Never," said Peter, "You shall never wash my feet."

Jesus replied, "If I do not wash you, you can have no share with me." Simon Peter said,

"Well then, Lord, not only my feet but my hands and head as well" (Jn 13:6-9).

It would seem a stupid question: "Lord, are you going to wash my feet?" Jesus had already begun to wash some of the other disciples' feet, so why not Simon's? Simon Peter has the tendency to think of himself as slightly different from the rest of the Twelve and who can blame him? Jesus has already renamed him, Cephas, meaning Rock. It is Simon who has the courage to speak out when many disciples decide to leave Jesus: "Lord, to whom shall we go? You have the message of eternal life, and we believe; we have come to know that you are the Holy One of God."[5]

It's a penchant we all have, to think ourselves different or set apart from others. We nod and agree at sermons directed at others in the parish, never for a moment considering they might be aimed at us: "Wonderful homily Father, but it wasn't about me."

We smile politely at the people rattling through the rosary after daily Mass, secure that we are contemplatives and don't need such repetition: "They go too fast. I prefer to pray alone." We stop our ears during the post-Communion rendition of *One Bread, One Body*, and focus on what we have just received: "I find it so distracting. I'm trying to commune with my Lord." We think we're different.

Jesus' response is ever patient: "At the moment you do not know what I am doing, but later you will understand." I was on retreat at a monastery a few years ago and I spoke to one of the older monks there. He was in his eighties. He told me that he remembered when he was sixteen, serving Mass. All of a sudden he had his first thought of vocation: "One day I'll be a priest like that." He wasn't ordained until the age of sixty-four, having spent most of his life as a missionary brother in India. It was when he embarked upon monastic life that he finally gave up the idea of being a priest. The day he resigned himself to being a lay-monk was the day the Abbot called to see him and asked him to serve the community as a priest. It was only at the end of his life that he could see how God had really been calling him to priesthood.

Very often in life we don't understand. Very often our prayers seem to go unheeded, our spiritual lives seem to lack direction. We can pray and pray and pray, and not get anywhere. And yet the conviction of our faith is that prayers are always heard and always answered. My father died when I was seventeen and I can remember praying in the hope that, if I opened my heart to God, somehow he would work something good out of this terrible tragedy. His reply was to implant in me the seeds of my vocation which I only fully accepted some years later. Sometimes it is only with hindsight that we can see God's response.

Whenever we read the Old Testament, we need to remember that what has been written down was once an oral tradition and before that perhaps a distant and historic event. Take the Exodus for example. The story of Moses leading the people of Israel from slavery in Egypt to freedom is clearly the work of years of reflection upon the actual event. It is later that we realise God's hand in what has happened. The essential truths of the account are not historical and factual, but theological. The fact that there was an exodus from Egypt is important; that it was God calling his people from bondage is more important.

God is with us and he does answer our prayers. Yet we try to second-guess his love for us. We try to determine his plan for us. We try to make God fit into our plans. He has none of it: *I am who I am.* One of the most important parts of discernment is letting go of our own preconceptions. Listen to God as he speaks to you, not as you want him to speak to you.

Gerard Hughes writes about the way God teaches us through our prayer. He says that we pray for self-centred things generally, such as wealth and success, or health and popularity. And yet we remain poor and a failure, or poorly and unpopular.

The temptation is to break off relations altogether. You must not. Grumble at God, complain at his unreasonableness, pester him with your complaints, keep fighting. God is like a loving mother who smiles as her child kicks and screams in her arms until sleep takes over. God teaches us through our tantrums.[6]

It seems to me that Jesus teaches Simon through his misunderstanding. Perhaps, to be fair to Simon Peter, he wasn't trying to assert his difference from the other disciples. "You will never wash my feet," he protests. Perhaps it was precisely his profound sense of who Jesus is that provokes his reaction. Perhaps he was saying, "There is no way the Anointed One is going to wash my feet. I should be washing *his* feet."

Whatever the motives, Simon gets it wrong. Jesus isn't interested in what we can do for him. God doesn't need us. Simon Peter is thinking really of himself, not Jesus. As Carlo Martini puts it:

His mistake lies in wanting to play the main part himself. Putting it theologically, we could say that he wants to save Jesus, he wants to be saviour of the Lord.[7]

We, too, often get it wrong. We misunderstand the love with which God loves us. We interpret it as some sort of demand made upon us, or else as some sort of privilege that no one else has. We become protective of our faith and our Church. Perhaps what is really behind Simon's actions is that somehow he feels he must earn his place of discipleship. We don't earn God's love, we simply have to let him love us; let him wash our feet.

Betrayal

Jesus said, "No one who has had a bath needs washing, such a person is clean all over. You too are clean, though not all of you are." He knew who was going to betray him, and that was why he said, "though not all of you are" (Jn 13:10-11).

It is a sobering thought that, after the intensity and emotion of the Last Supper, Judas goes out to betray Jesus. I often wonder how much this betrayal must have hurt Christ at a personal level. One of the Twelve, one of his closest companions for the past three years, hands him over to be executed.

The only betrayal I have known is the betrayal of confidences once or twice from friends I thought I could trust. I know of others who have felt really stabbed in the back – people who have been ripped off in business by old friends; people who have been conned; people who have been let down at a crucial time; married people deceived by their partners. The pain lies in the personal nature of the perfidy. The psalmist captures the emotions well:

Were it an enemy who insulted me,
that I could bear;
if an opponent pitted himself against me,
I could turn away from him.

But you, a person of my own rank,
a comrade and dear friend,
to whom I was bound by intimate friendship
in the house of God (Ps 55:12-14).

The word 'betrayal' has its roots in the Latin, *tradere*, meaning to hand over. This same word gives us the notion of Tradition – that transmission of the good news of salvation. We find the concept again in John's Gospel when Pilate hands Jesus over to be crucified. Whereas Tradition denotes a handing on of something shared, betrayal implies a handing over and thereby a letting go. Judas, then, in betraying Christ is essentially letting go of his relationship with him. Betrayal means rejection.

The Catholic Church has always made rather sensible differentiation of sins. Some dislike the categories of mortal and venial since all sin is a falling short of our true vocation. The biblical notion of 'missing the mark' would seem more appropriate. But sins do vary in their seriousness. A white lie is not a premeditated murder. We miss the mark by varying degrees. Which sins, then, constitute a betrayal? Which sins represent our handing over of the Christ, our letting go of the relationship?

I find the theological tool of the 'fundamental option' useful here. Am I, at my fundamental core of being, directed towards or away from God? In other words, am I for him or against him? Are my sins symptomatic of the struggle against God or the struggle for him? Peter denies Christ three times. "I do not know him," he protests to the woman in Luke's Gospel (Lk 22:57). Indeed Peter, after all that time, still doesn't know the Lord. But he is *coming* to know him. Although he follows the arrested Jesus at a distance, at least he follows him. What of my sins, my denials? Am I basically going in the same direction as Jesus, or am I heading off on my own?

What is incredible about the Christian message is that even betrayal can be forgiven. Even the radical rejection of relationship with God is not the end. Unlike his betrayers, God remains loyal and open. In the parable of the Prodigal Son, the Father doesn't count the cost of the young boy's squandering. He merely rejoices that his son has come back home. The handing over of a share of the estate at the beginning of the story symbolises the rejection of the family. The young son is going to go his own way and be his own man. No family ties. It is as if the Father knows how it will end and simply waits with patience. Sooner or later the boy will realise that he can't go it alone.

Another sobering thought is how the rest of the Twelve behave. We know that Judas betrays him and that Peter denies him. As if this were not enough, James and John argue about who is the greatest, and Thomas doubts his resurrection. All of them run away, leaving only John to stand at Calvary. Yet Jesus had invested so much time and energy in them. According to Luke's Gospel, he spent the whole night in prayer before appointing them (Lk 6:12-16). How could Jesus get it so wrong?

There are two obvious implications for us. Firstly, God's love calls weak and sinful human beings to be disciples. God offers us the way of salvation: the way to become bigger and more human than we are at the moment. For all their faults, the Twelve are promised by Christ that they will eat and drink at his table in his kingdom.[8] And if we think about the disciples' courage and martyrdom after Pentecost, we tend to revise our opinion of them. As Jesus replies to his critics, "I have come to call not the upright but sinners to repentance (Lk 5:32).

The second implication is that prayer isn't the ready-made solution to all our problems in the way that we would like to think it is. It doesn't take away our responsibility to act, or our ability to make mistakes. Prayer is not about calling upon a heavenly Mr Fix-It to sort out our day-to-day anxieties. It does not stop us being human and being fallible. If we look at Jesus' prayer in the garden of Gethsemane, he asks to be saved from death and yet goes on to die upon the cross.

> *Some time later came the resurrection through which he entered a state where death could never again be on the remotest horizon… A prayer to be saved from death is answered by the gift of eternal freedom from death beyond the wildest dreams of the petitioner.*[9]

Prayer, then, is about the Kingdom. Prayer for healing, prayer to be more fully alive, prayer for the forgiveness of sins: these are the prayers of the true disciple. Not praying to win the lottery, or to find a fiver stuffed in your coat pocket. What prayer does do is ensure that in the long run we remain open to the love of God.

Service

When he had washed their feet and put on his outer garments again he went back to the table. "Do you understand what I have done to you? You call me Master and Lord, and rightly; so I am. If I, then, the Lord and Master, have washed your feet, you must wash each other's feet. I have given you an example so that you may copy what I have done to you (Jn 13:12-15).

One of my favourite parts of the Easter Triduum is the washing of feet on Maundy Thursday during the Mass of the Lord's Supper. Once a year the priest, who for so much of the time is seen to lead worship, to make decisions, to hold the power in the parish, kneels down before his people and copies Christ's example. It is an image that we should carry with us throughout the year. Our life of discipleship is a life to be spent imitating Christ. A life of trying to love as we are loved.

As a priest, I am always struck when I say the words at Mass: "This is the cup of my blood, the blood of the new and everlasting covenant. It will be shed for you and for all." I wonder if I will be called to shed my blood for those I serve. It reminds me of those Jesuits who were shot along with their housekeeper in South America a few years ago simply because they spoke out against injustice.

When we celebrate the Eucharist, we are invited to reflect on the vision of service that Jesus gives us. Do we serve? Do we love others? Do we really care about anyone but ourselves? Are we willing to lay down our lives for those around us? Or has our love become something locked up inside of us? As Jesus promised the Samaritan woman at the well, the love that he gives us is not something static, but a spring, welling up within us and overflowing to all around. "I have given you an example," says the Lord. Let our resolution be to follow that example with all our heart.

NOTES

1. Bishops' Conference of England and Wales, *The Sign We Give. Report from the Working Party on Collaborative Ministry*, Matthew James Publishing Ltd., 1995, p. 17.
2. *See* Exodus 3:14 in Revised Standard Version. Interestingly in the *New Jerusalem Bible* it is translated as "I am he who is".
3. Cf. T. Merton, *The Seven Story Mountain*, London, 1975, pp. 285-286.
4. *See* John 19:23-24.
5. *See* John 1:42 and 6:67-69.
6. G. Hughes, *Knocking on Heaven's Door*, in *The Tablet*, 21 February 1998, pp. 247-8.
7. C. Martini, (trans. Susan Leslie), *Ministers of the Gospel. Meditations on St Luke's Gospel*, St Pauls Publishing, 1983, p. 69.
8. *See* Luke 22:28-30.
9. K. Collins, *The Prayer of Jesus*, in *The Unsealed Fountain*, Oscott Series 1, Veritas, p. 36.

3
The Cost of Discipleship

Reflections on the Crucifixion
Mark 15:33-39

You are in trouble this day;
then I am in trouble.
Another is in trouble tomorrow;
then I am in trouble.
After this generation, other descendants,
who will succeed your descendants, are in trouble;
then I am in trouble.
Down to the end of the world,
whoever is in trouble,
then I am in trouble.

(St Augustine, on Psalm 102)

Inevitability

One of them, Caiaphas, the high priest that year, said, "You do not seem to have grasped the situation at all; you fail to see that it is to your advantage that one man should die for the people, rather than the whole nation should perish" (Jn 11:49-50).

On Monday 24th March 1980, Oscar Romero, the Archbishop of San Salvador, was shot dead as he celebrated Mass. The Gospel which had been read only moments earlier was from John 12:23-26: "Unless a grain of wheat falls into the earth and dies, it remains only a single grain." Sometime before his death, the Archbishop had said: "Those who get in the way get killed." Romero had got in the way.

In the gospels too there is an air of inevitability about Jesus' passion and death. In each of the Synoptics there are three Passion predictions. In John there is the 'Hour'. The moment of Christ's death is a climax to the whole of his public ministry.

We know the circumstances and context of Jesus' execution. Jerusalem was occupied by the Romans. In Galilee there was the half-Jewish puppet royal family led by Herod. In Palestine, Pontius Pilate was the Roman governor. The Chief Priests and Temple officials were sitting uneasily with the Roman authorities, negotiating compromises, trying to ensure relative religious freedom for the Jews;

above all to preserve the Temple from defilement or destruction. We also know that the times were highly charged. Barabbas, who was released in place of Jesus, was a leading figure with the Zealots – a group of terrorists committed to overthrowing the Romans by force. We know too that there was a real mix of Messianic expectation among the people. People are on edge. It is the season of Passover. Jerusalem is heaving with pilgrims. Will Jesus come up for the festival or not? Is this the moment of Jewish self-determination and freedom? As John the Baptist had asked earlier, "Are you the one who is to come, or are we to expect another?" (Lk 7:19). Finally, we know there were the different Jewish religious groups: Pharisees, Scribes, Sadducees – all playing for control of the Sanhedrin.

What of Jesus himself? To the Jewish leaders he was a revolutionary. A popular, powerful preacher who seemed to disregard the delicate politics of the time. An uncompromising rabbi who took it upon himself to reinterpret the Law, and to break it when he felt it necessary. To the people, he was like the prophets of old, speaking out against the hypocrisy of their leaders. One who would stand up for the poor, and condemn injustice and some of the oppressive and arcane religious practices that tied them up. To the outcasts, the prostitutes, tax-collectors, and other sinners, Jesus was a figure of hope and acceptance; but one who demanded conversion. To the Romans he was insignificant; perhaps a potential rabble-rouser. To all he was controversial. He purged the Temple and broke the Sabbath. He preached love of enemies and refused to openly condemn the Roman occupation. Ultimately, like Oscar Romero, he began to get in the way.

Jon Sobrino, a Jesuit theologian working in South America, sums up the inevitability of Jesus' arrest and crucifixion:

Jesus, surrounded by conflict, got in the way, in the last resort because he got in the way of other gods, other idols, and did so in the name of God.[1]

In other words, Jesus was put to death because he would not compromise his relationship with his Father. The Kingdom was everything for Jesus: that vision and making real of God's love for all of us. But the Kingdom, once it is proclaimed, inevitably comes up against hostility and sin.

What of our lives and our proclamation of God's Kingdom? Do we share the uncompromising vision that Jesus held? Do we speak up for the oppressed, react against injustice, demonstrate love for all, and touch the untouchable? Does selfishness and self-interest fear our advent? Does evil flee before us? Do we face opposition and hostility because of our faith?

A text which seems to me to be almost always misinterpreted is that of Matthew 16:18:

So I now say to you: You are Peter, and on this rock I will build my community. And the gates of the underworld can never overpower it.

Mostly people assume that this secures the Church from the onslaught of hell. It's as if Jesus were saying, "Batten down the hatches, you'll be okay. Hell won't harm you." In fact Jesus' words are far more powerful and positive than this. The Revised Standard Version of the same text uses the word 'prevail' in place of 'overpower'. What Jesus is actually saying is that it is hell which must run for cover. The onslaught comes from the Kingdom and the Kingdom will win.

How do we reconcile this, then, with the apparent triumphs of evil? Jesus preached the Kingdom and the world crucified him. Innocent people are put to death. In our own century we need only think of the Holocaust. As many theologians put it, how can we do theology after Auschwitz? As Sobrino asks from his situation of violent oppression in South America, how can we do theology *in* Auschwitz?[2]

Jesus' life and death show us one thing quite clearly: that Christ's message and the workings of the world are in conflict. The world demands compromise and sell-out. It encourages and looks for self-interest. Christ demands uncompromising love. The crucifixion is inevitable for Jesus. Time, history, society, religion, politics – everything conspires against him. The sin that asserted itself in Genesis is not going to tolerate a saviour. The sin of pride and self-love will not surrender itself to the grace of being loved without a fight. I often think that if Jesus had come in our own time we would still have crucified him. A theologian such as Sobrino would argue that in South America, with all the oppression and injustice, we are in the process of crucifying him.

The inevitability of Jesus' cross should be an inevitability for us too. Jesus said to his disciples, "If the world hates you, you must realise that it hated me before it hated you," and again, "If they persecuted me, they will persecute you too."[3] We must not think that our discipleship differs in any great degree to those who are glorified as martyrs. A sign that we are following Christ is that we encounter opposition to his message. We are called to hold on to the promise made in Matthew 16:18, and to trust that ultimately evil is on the run.

Compassion

While the Jews demand miracles and the Greeks look for wisdom, we are preaching a crucified Christ: to the Jews an obstacle they cannot get over, to the gentiles foolishness, but to those who have been called, whether they are Jews or Greeks, a Christ who is both the power of God and the wisdom of God (1 Cor 1:22-24).

I remember watching a television interview with a survivor of the Holocaust. The man continues to observe Judaism but has completely lost his faith in God. His experiences in Auschwitz have led him to conclude there cannot be a God. If there is a God – one who could have allowed such atrocities to happen – then who would want anything to do with him? Asked why he still follows the Jewish faith, he replied that to give up Judaism would be to let the Nazis win.

The horrors of the concentration camps such as Auschwitz and Bergen are modern day icons of the absence of God. Symbols, should we need them, not only of the presence of evil but also of its power. The question, how to do theology after Auschwitz is an important one. Where was God when millions of innocent men, women, and children were being massacred in the pursuit of some perverted ideal?

The cross at the time of Jesus carried with it a similar iconic horror. It operated at two levels. At the purely human level, crucifixion was a slow, painful death. A public display of the power of the authorities and what would happen should anyone oppose them. Having been beaten, stripped of his garments, led through the crowds and ridiculed, Jesus was nailed and bound to a cross and hung out to die: to become nothing more than a pathetic carcass hanging on a gibbet. At this level, crucifixion was the destruction of everything human. At a theological level, the cross was a symbol of hell. There was, at that time, a Jewish tradition that if someone were hung from a tree outside of the city walls it was a clear sign to all that God had abandoned them. The cross of Jesus stood outside the city walls of Jerusalem.

There is a scene in the film, *Schindler's List*, when the concentration camp commandant gets out of bed one morning, goes out to his balcony overlooking the camp, takes his rifle, and begins to shoot down Jews as if they were pigeons. The revulsion of the act is brought out by the bored manner in which he executes at random: women, children, the elderly. Not only are his actions abhorrent, but there is a repulsion in his very physical slobbishness, as it is offset by the panic and frantic movement of his victims below. We are presented in this scene with a fundamental truth about Nazism: it denied that Jews were really human. They were considered nothing more than vermin.

What was happening in the Holocaust was more than just genocide. It was the denial of both God and humanity. The Jews were seen as subhuman, something to be despised and destroyed. But who are the Jews if not God's Chosen People? What was the Holocaust if not the attempt to eradicate the *Qahal Yahweh*, and to stamp out faith in God as well? An interview with Rabbi Jonathan Sacks makes the point:

> *The real question isn't where was God in Auschwitz, but where was man at Auschwitz? God was there in the command, "Thou shalt not murder." God was there in the command, "Thou shalt not oppress a stranger." God was at Auschwitz in the words, "Thy brother's blood cried out to me from the ground." At Auschwitz, God spoke, and humanity didn't listen.*[4]

In the Holocaust the irony was that, in attempting to rid the world of the People of God, the Nazis themselves became inhuman and Godless.

There is another dimension to the horrors of both the crucifixion and the Holocaust: the dimension of original sin. Pious language often talks about how our sins have nailed Jesus to the cross. I cringe at such sentiments but I cannot disagree. As human beings we have a collective responsibility for the crimes of humanity. A monk once advised me: "Never be surprised at the depths to which we as humans can sink."

I often wonder about those soldiers, doctors, and bureaucrats who found themselves caught up in the Holocaust. Not only the Germans but the Jews who found themselves placed in charge of other Jews and collaborated with what was going on. I wonder about the civilians involved – profiteers like Oskar

Schindler, out to make himself a fortune. I wonder, how would I have reacted at the time? Am I actually any different when it comes to the crunch? Surely the basic instincts of self-survival and greed are as powerful in me? In the film, *Schindler's List*, Schindler starts out as nothing other that an apathetic businessman. His motives are profit and greed rather than any desire to save. He is blind to the real horrors of what is going on as he pursues his ambition of exploitation and wealth. Yet something changes him; by the end he is an uncompromising saviour.

Recently there was shown a documentary entitled, *Owning Auschwitz*. It followed the claims by a Jew that the land on which Auschwitz had been built was originally, and legally still, Jewish. In fact part of it belonged to the woman herself. Early on in the film we were shown the woman's elation as she calculated how much she could make from a row of garages on the site. To be fair, she did insist that she had no interest in actually possessing the land, just to let its origins and true ownership be known. But as Tom Sutcliffe put it,

> *Her appetite for profit had seemed inappropriate to the solemnity of the occasion but suddenly you were aware that your feelings might be continuous with far more dangerous prejudices, far less admissible distastes.*[5]

The documentary cleverly led us into the arena of our own prejudices and racism and then presented us with real anti-Semitism, at which we recoiled. The point it was making was that we weren't so far removed from those attitudes that made the Holocaust possible. For me, it made me acknowledge once again my need for a Redeemer.

I believe, then, that for Jesus' disciples the cross held a similar horrific significance to that which places such as Auschwitz hold for us today. What convinces me of the fact of the resurrection is that the disciples somehow make sense of this crucifixion. The icon of death and hell is preached as the symbol of love and eternal life. This could not happen unless the cross was not the end. Imagine a survivor of the Holocaust pointing to Bergen and saying, "This is the sign of God's love." Without resurrection such sentiments are a nonsense. And so we have St Paul saying that the message of the cross is folly. Of course it is, unless you believe in the resurrection. One of the problems today is that the sign of the cross has lost that shock value. We have produced in jewellery an image of a dead man hanging from a gibbet and we think nothing of it.

One of the images we are given for the feast of Christ the King is the crucifixion. The telling line is that of the Good Thief, who says, "Jesus, remember me when you come into your kingdom." It is significant that at the moment of Jesus' death a criminal also dying with him should recognise him as a king. In art we often find Christ robed in kingly attire, yet crucified. The cross is precisely the moment of his reign.

On the cross we see not just man, but God. The very icon of death and destruction, of hell and despair is turned around. What symbolises the absence of God and the end of human life now becomes the place where God reigns and eternal life begins. God, in Christ, fills the moment of hell with his divine love. Now death, hell, despair has no territory or symbol to claim its own.

Our Christian hope is based upon this crucifixion. Since Christ has filled God-forsakenness with God's presence, there can now be no place where God is said to be absent. The modern day *loci* of hell, such as the Holocaust, such as innocent suffering – even these can become the vehicle for God's reign. Where we would want to say God has abandoned us, our faith insists that God is there, present, suffering with us. Compassion means precisely this: to suffer with. And as we assert with the psalmist: The Lord is compassion and love (Ps 103).

Jon Sobrino sums up what I am trying to say here with his own personal experience:

On 16 November 1989, when the Jesuits of the Central American University were murdered outside their house, the body of Juan Ramón Moreno was dragged inside the residence into one of the rooms, mine. In the movement one book from the bookcase in the room fell on to the floor and became soaked in Juan Ramón's blood. That book was 'The Crucified God'. It is a symbol, of course, but it expresses... God's real participation in the passion of the world.[6]

Evil is something very real and can take hold of our hearts. As in the Holocaust and as with the crucifixion, it attempts to wipe out both human goodness and Godliness. But the message of the cross is unambiguous: since God is with us even in the horror and suffering of oppression, evil cannot ultimately triumph. As St Paul writes,

> *For I am certain of this: neither death nor life, nor angels, nor principalities, nothing already in existence and nothing still to come, nor any power, nor the heights nor the depths, nor any created thing whatever, will be able to come between us and the love of God, known to us in Christ Jesus our Lord* (Rom 8:38-39).

Whereas humanity may abandon its God and let evil begin to reign, God does not abandon humanity, but will rather chose to suffer with his people.

Darkness

When the sixth hour came there was darkness over the whole land until the ninth hour (Mk 15:33).

There is a scene in C. S. Lewis' novel, *The Lion, the Witch, and the Wardrobe*, when the Lion, Aslan, is sacrificed upon the Table of Stone. The Witch and all her cronies have gathered together and are moving in for the kill: this is the moment of their triumph.

This line of Mark's Gospel has similar connotations. Jesus has mounted the wood of the cross and now a darkness descends over the whole land, until his death. Yet Mark tells us it is the sixth hour: midday – supposedly the brightest part of the day. Mark seems to be underlining the drama of what is about to happen. It is as if all the forces of evil and darkness are amassing for their moment of victory: to claim the death of someone truly innocent.

St Paul speaks of the whole of creation groaning in travail, awaiting its glorious liberty.[7] With the advent of darkness and the moment of Christ's death, it seems that the whole of creation enters into the tragedy. The darkness symbolises a sort of universal despair at what is happening.

Darkness is a symbol often used. Writers tell of the dark night of the soul to express that dry and barren prayer, devoid of any consolation. People speak of the darkness of depression or mental illness. We say someone has a 'dark state of mind' at the moment. In St John's Gospel, much is made of people preferring darkness to light. When Judas leaves the Last Supper to betray Jesus we are told night has fallen.[8]

We find in John's Gospel and Ephesians the Christian response of hope to all forms of darkness. The Prologue to the fourth gospel states clearly: "Light shines in the darkness, and darkness could not overpower it" (Jn 1:5). The Letter to the Ephesians says: "You were darkness once, but now you are light in the Lord" (Eph 5:8). There is a confidence that the moments of despair and darkness are merely illusory. Christ our Light has triumphed. This boldness is echoed in the beginning of the Easter Vigil, when, in the darkened church, *Lumen Christi* is solemnly proclaimed three times. Again, in the *Exsultet*, we sing of the Risen Saviour shining upon us and of Christ the Morning Star that never sets. An ancient sermon from St Maximus of Turin expresses this confidence well:

The light of Christ is day without night, day without end... Just as there is no night at all to follow the heavenly day, so too the darkness of sin does not follow the justice of Christ... The brilliance and the flashing radiance of Christ's light never cease, and there is no darkness of sin which can overcome them.[9]

In the *Nania* story, the Lion returns from death and explains to the children that there lay a deeper magic which the Witch and her evil cronies had forgotten. C. S. Lewis' story is, of course, a parable for the salvation of the cross. On Calvary, Christ shone into the darkness of despair and death and dispelled it once and for all. The light of Love is a deeper magic, if you like, than the darkness of destruction and evil.

The last words

And at the ninth hour Jesus cried out in a loud voice, "Eloi, Eloi, lama sabachthani?" which means, "My God, my God, why have you forsaken me?" When some of those who stood by heard this, they said, "Listen, he is calling on Elijah." Someone there ran and soaked a sponge in vinegar and, putting it on a reed, gave it to him to drink, saying, "Wait and see if Elijah will come to take him down" (Mk 15:33-36).

"*Eloi, Eloi, lama sabachthani?*" are the last words of Jesus recorded by St Mark. They mirror those in Matthew's Gospel, although Matthew uses the Hebrew, *Eli, Eli,* in place of the Aramaic used here. They are, of course, the opening words of Psalm 22:

My God, my God, why have you forsaken me?
The words of my groaning do nothing to save me.
My God, I call by day but you do not answer,
at night, but I find no respite.

This is the cry of a man abandoned. There is nothing serene here. This is the call of someone in total darkness. "Where are you God? Why have you left me?" We all struggle with our faith at times and most of us have probably echoed these words at some point in our lives.

It is true that Psalm 22 finishes with hope and confidence. I don't think we should use that as an excuse to take away from the anguish of Jesus' passion. Often phrases of psalms come to mind which capture our mood at that moment. It doesn't mean we're necessarily aware of the sentiment of the whole psalm. There is a tendency not to want to allow the Christ to suffer. There is a tendency to over stress his divinity to the detriment of his humanity. To view the cross as some sort of stage-piece drama of God's love, but not a real, painful, anguished death. Yet that is precisely what it was: agony, abandonment, darkness. If we take these away from Christ's experience then we water down the power of his sacrifice. Having said that, the end lines of Psalm 22 are remarkable:

The whole world will remember and return to Yahweh,
all the families of nations bow before him.
For to Yahweh, ruler of the nations,
belongs kingly power!
All who prosper on earth will bow before him,
all who go down to the dust will do reverence before him.
And those who are dead, their descendants will serve him,
will proclaim his name to generations still to come;
and these will tell of his saving justice to a people yet unborn: he has fulfilled it.

For me, these lines sum up the efficacy of the cross. Through Christ's death, the power of God's love is proclaimed throughout the world and to all generations. What began as abandonment and

God-forsakenness has become the fulfilment of saving justice. On the cross Christ shows himself to be Universal King, reigning in the place where previously even God was thought to be absent.

In Luke's Gospel, Jesus' last words are the cry of final resignation: "Father, into your hands I commend my spirit" (Lk 23:46). At Jesus' baptism, which marked the beginning of his public ministry, the voice of God the Father was heard, saying, "You are my son" (Lk 3:22). At the end of his public ministry the cry of Jesus is heard, calling out, 'Father'. These two voices bracket Jesus' ministry in this gospel. At the start there is the divine initiative: the Father expressing his love for the Son. At the end there is the response of the Son, handing back everything to the Father. In between, with the public ministry, there is the demonstration of this Father-Son relationship.

At our baptism we became adopted sons and daughters of God the Father. We became co-heirs with Christ to the Kingdom. Although we didn't physically hear it, the love of the Father was expressed as he called us, 'My son' or 'My daughter'. Essentially the journey of discipleship is about a listening for that divine initiative. It is about responding and calling out, 'Father', and meaning it with all our heart, with all our soul, and with all our might. My own prayer is that, at the end of my life, my last words will echo those of Christ: "Father, into your hands I commend my spirit."

There is passion in these last words too. Jesus calls upon his Father but this time there is no response, only silence. How often do we come up against this silence? How often do we cry out, 'Father', and seemingly meet only a brick wall of indifference? At least we know that Jesus has been there before us.

In John's Gospel, the last words are recorded as: "It is fulfilled." Some translations use the expression, 'finished', or 'accomplished'.[10] Jesus has fulfilled and accomplished the will of God. He did not stint or compromise. He remained true to the Kingdom and showed a love prepared to give itself up in death. A person of total commitment and integrity. In John's Gospel, Jesus' public ministry is now finished as he returns to his Father. With the resurrection will come the new age of the Spirit.

Sacred and profane

But Jesus gave a loud cry and breathed his last. And the veil of the Sanctuary was torn in two from top to bottom. The centurion, who was standing in front of him, had seen how he had died, and he said, "In truth this man was Son of God" (Mk 15:37-39).

We have here a cry of anguish, a man's death, and a pagan soldier's act of faith. The Roman centurion – one of the hated occupiers of the Holy Land – is the first to pronounce the significance of Jesus' death. This man must have witnessed hundreds of crucifixions. Yet in the darkness, with the tearing of the Temple veil, it is almost like an extraordinary clarity of vision comes through: this man was Son of God.

The veil divided the Holy of Holies off from the Holy Place, all within the sanctuary of the Temple. Only the priests would enter the Holy of Holies at certain times of the year. With the tearing of the veil at Jesus' death we have the clear signal that there is now no one place of divine indwelling. St Paul takes this up when he speaks about us having become temples of the Holy Spirit.[11] With his one, eternal sacrifice on the cross, Jesus has replaced the cultic sacrifices of the Jewish temple. With his reigning from the cross, the symbol of Godlessness, Jesus has put an end to the division between what is sacred and what is profane. Now everything is a possible vehicle for the sacred.

The pagan soldier's act of faith underpins this. Gentiles were the embodiment of all that was profane. Jews were the people set apart by God: his holy ones. With Jesus' death it is the heathen, not the holy one, who first proclaims the truth of salvation.

NOTES

1. J. Sobrino, *Jesus the Liberator*, p. 196.
2. *Ibid.*, p. 195.
3. *See* John 15:18-24.
4. This was given in an interview with Deborah Ross in *The Independent* on 4 May 1998.
5. Tom Sutcliffe is a television critic for *The Independent*. He wrote this on 21 April 1998.
6. J. Sobrino, *Jesus the Liberator*, p. 235.
7. *See* Romans 8:18-23.
8. *See* John 1:4-5; 3:19-21; 13:30.
9. Cf. Maximus of Turin, *Sermon* 53:1-2, 4
10. John 19:30. Cf. *New Jerusalem Bible*, Revised Standard Version, and Jerusalem translation.
11. 1 Corinthians 6:19: *Do you not realise that your body is the temple of the Holy Spirit, who is in you and whom you received from God?*

4
The Call to Holiness

Reflections on the Invitation of
Isaiah 55:1-3, 6-11

*The tree of life my soul has seen,
Laden with fruit and always green:
The trees of nature fruitless be
Compared with Christ the apple tree.*

(Anon., collection of Joshua Smith,
New Hampshire, 1784)

Come and eat

Oh, come to the water all you who are thirsty;
though you have no money, come!
Buy and eat; come, buy wine and milk
without money, free!
Why spend money on what cannot nourish
and your wages on what fails to satisfy?
Listen carefully to me, and you will have
good things to eat
and rich food to enjoy.
Pay attention, come to me;
listen, and you will live (Is 55:1-3).

With these lines from Isaiah we have an invitation to the banquet of new life. This is the new age when money, merit, poverty, and death will have no more place. The call is open to all: "Come, buy wine and milk without money, free!" The only condition is that we have a thirst for God.

One of my favourite stories is *The Great Divorce*, by C. S. Lewis. The title itself might seem curious, since the novel is about a day trip to heaven. Souls languishing in purgatory take a bus to heaven and, if they like it, they can stay. If not, they make the return journey and purgatory becomes hell. The title refers to the ultimate chasm that must exist between what is of God and what it not. As Lewis says in his preface,

If we insist on keeping Hell (or even earth) we

shall not see Heaven: if we accept Heaven we shall not be able to retain even the smallest and most intimate souvenirs of Hell.[1]

The 'catch', for those souls who wish to stay in heaven, is that they must give up completely their trophies. They must give up what they possess or what possesses them. The following extract demonstrates what C. S. Lewis was getting at. The narrator has taken the day-trip and watched a number of encounters between the trippers – portrayed as shadowy ghosts for whom even the grass of heaven is so real it cuts their through their feet – and the Solid Ones, those who have given up looking at themselves and are making their way into the mountains of heaven. Here, the narrator asks why some chose to go back to hell rather than to stay in heaven:

> *"In the actual language of the Lost, the words will be different, no doubt. One will say he has always served his country right or wrong; and another that he has sacrificed everything to his Art; and some that they've never been taken in, and some, thank God, they've always looked after Number One, and nearly all, that, at least they've been true to themselves."*
> *"And the Saved?"*
> *"Ah, the Saved...what happens to them is best described as the opposite of a mirage. What seemed, when they entered it, to be a vale of misery turns out, when they look back, to have been a well; and where present experience saw*

only salt deserts, memory truthfully records that the pools were full of water."

"Then those people are right who say that Heaven and Hell are only states of mind?"

"Hush," said he sternly. "Do not blaspheme. Hell is a state of mind – ye never said a truer word. And every state of mind, left to itself, every shutting up of the creature within the dungeon of its own mind – is, in the end, Hell. But Heaven is not a state of mind. Heaven is reality itself."[2]

For C. S. Lewis, the choosing of heaven consists precisely in the letting go of self and self-props and allowing our essential need and desire for God to become evident. In the words of Isaiah, it means thirsting for God and so being able to take up that invitation to the heavenly banquet.

The image of thirsting is one we find again and again in the Scriptures. It was Jesus' thirst, remember, that began the encounter with the Samaritan woman at the well and led on to the revelation of the deeper thirst of the woman for salvation. The image of the heavenly banquet is similarly a common scriptural theme and one taken up in the theology of the Mass. In Isaiah, the banquet promised is of 'good things to eat' and of 'rich food to enjoy'. The heavenly banquet which will quench our thirst is the reality; our thirsting and earthly food and drink a mere shadow. We are promised riches and nourishment beyond belief. Yet the irony of our sin is that we want to cling to what we think satisfies us or keeps us going.

St Paul uses the terminology of the 'spiritual body' in his letter to the Corinthians. The point he makes is that Resurrection life is *real* life – a reality which we can but glimpse in our present state. The life we now lead is only a vestige of the eternal life promised us.

> *The sun has its own splendour, the moon another splendour, and the stars yet another splendour; and the stars differ among themselves in splendour. It is the same too with the resurrection of the dead: what is sown is perishable, but what is raised is imperishable; what is sown is contemptible but what is raised is glorious; what is sown is weak, but what is raised is powerful; what is sown is a natural body, and what is raised is a spiritual body* (1 Cor 15:41-44).

Yet we choose to hold on to these shadows and vestiges. We would go on scraping for earthly nourishment and fulfilment rather than accept the invitation to real food and drink.

The call to holiness is made: "Pay attention, come to me; listen and you will live." To pay attention to God means ridding ourselves of those other things that hold our desires. The life of discipleship is a journey made in response to that call of Isaiah. Gradually, following the example of love given by Christ, and daily accepting the cost that he accepted, we let go of self and become ever more real.

Seek the Lord

Seek out Yahweh while he is still to be found,
call to him while he is still near.
Let the wicked abandon his way
and the evil one his thoughts.
Let him turn back to Yahweh who will take
pity on him,
to our God, for he is rich in forgiveness;
for my thoughts are not your thoughts
and your ways are not my ways,
declares Yahweh.
For the heavens are as high above earth
as my ways are above your ways,
my thoughts above your thoughts (Is 55:6-9).

An image I have of purgatory is of a hospital waiting area. Sitting with me are old friends and people I knew, even people I never really liked. At first no one talks much. Then, suddenly, a doctor enters and says he will see to us in a moment. In the meantime we are to strip down in separate cubicles and wait. The doctor seems familiar to all of us and this breaks the ice. We begin to speak. Who is he? Where do we know him from? Suddenly there is a camaraderie even amongst former enemies. I have my suspicions and I reckon others have too. But none of us will say it: "It is the Lord." I go into my cubicle, but I do not take my clothes off. I am embarrassed and I begin to doubt the doctor. Why do I need to be naked? Who is he *really*? Why am I here at all? The doctor returns and enters my section. At once I feel a fool. Now I know it is him and I wish I was naked before him. His response is a loving laugh. "I see you're not quite ready," he says and out he goes.

The image of nakedness is one which helps me understand why I need to go further along the journey of discipleship. It is an image which for me unites the first sin of Adam with the sacrifice of Christ. Adam sins and covers his nakedness. Christ dies on the cross, naked for all to see. In the garden of Eden, Adam hides when God approaches. In the garden of Gethsemane, Jesus visibly expresses his openness to the Father: "Let your will be done, not mine."[3] I still tend toward Adam rather than Christ. It is only when we are prepared to stand fully naked before our Creator that we are ready to let him love us. It is only when we allow God's love to take hold of every aspect of our being that we can enter paradise.

"Seek out Yahweh while he is still to be found," sums up the ambiguity of our world. We are bombarded every day with different values, different kingdoms, all vying for our attention. The call to holiness is a call to seek out God. To some this searching is expressed outward – a trawling through different traditions and theologies, a taste and see approach. To others, the journey is inward – an inner spiral to find God already present in the depths of our being. Both are essentially the same journey. Both face the same danger: in searching for God we can take on a lesser substitute. We can clothe ourselves in theologies and traditions; in gurus and self, rather than the Lord.

The true contemplative is one who finds God in each moment. One who has a sense of the divine constantly to mind. A true contemplative is one who stands naked in prayer before his Lord; unabashed and unashamed, letting himself be loved in all his imperfection. In her autobiography, Ruth Burrows says that she expects to be imperfect until the end of her life and yet she is certain that God's plan will be fulfilled in her. These sentiments express a letting go of 'doing' things for God and a realisation that true holiness is about God 'doing' things in us. We have nothing to offer but ourselves, empty and naked.

Isaiah urges us to call to the Lord while he is still near, abandoning our wicked ways and evil thoughts. The word, 'abandon', means to give up or forsake. It can also mean to yield oneself to another's control or mercy. So Charles de Foucauld prayed: "Father, I abandon myself into your hands, do with me what you will." When I was first ordained, I was given a diocesan car to get around in. It was new and certainly larger than I really needed. I'd only had it a week when someone said to me, "Well, you'd hardly get that through the eye of a needle." Although it was a joke, it hit a nerve. I was acutely aware of my materialism – in fact, I still am. When I told another friend the story, she simply shrugged and said, "You'll just have to throw yourself at the Divine Mercy, like the rest of us." The point she was making was far more apt than I dared to realise. It wouldn't be a diocesan car that would prevent me from entering paradise, but rather the thought that I could make my own way there. We, all of us, need to abandon ourselves to God.

The life of discipleship seems to me a series of constant surprises; a set of constant illuminations – a continual, "Oh, so that's it", if you like. We are reminded "My thoughts are not your thoughts, and your ways are not my ways", declares Yahweh. How true that is. What a mess salvation would be if I were in charge. I often think, when I'm being pestered by someone I can't stand, how odd it will be to go to heaven and find them already there. But what is even odder is that I will want them to be there; I will rejoice that they are with me.

Stop and listen

For, as the rain and the snow come down
from the sky
and do not return before having watered the earth,
fertilising it and making it germinate
to provide seed for the sower and food to eat,
so it is with the word that goes from my mouth:
it will not return to me unfulfilled
or before having carried out my good pleasure
and having achieved what it was sent to do
(Is 55:10-11).

One of the suggestions of Jesus that perhaps we most ignore in the Church is not to babble in our prayers. Sometimes I feel that the prayers of the Office and the Mass get caught up in their own poetry and forget about God. Often I feel that my own personal prayers are like that. Not that I pray poetically, I don't. But I do start to pray without any real meaning: I babble. Even in more meditative prayer, I'm aware that often I am day-dreaming or navel-gazing. A Benedictine once advised me: "When you find yourself distracted, simply raise your eyes to heaven and pray, "Thank God, thank God, thank God." What else can prayer be about?"

An exercise that is often done in school retreats is to ask the students to design their own coat of arms and to explain what each of the symbols they choose mean. They also have to decide a motto for themselves. A favourite of mine would be the beginning of Psalm 127: "If Yahweh does not build a house." The first two verses of the Psalm are as follows:

> *If Yahweh does not build a house*
> *in vain do its builders toil.*
> *If Yahweh does not guard a city*
> *in vain does its guard keep watch.*
>
> *In vain you get up earlier,*
> *and put off going to bed,*
> *sweating to make a living,*
> *since it is he who provides for his beloved*
> *as they sleep* (Ps 127:1-2).

The psalmist here captures the essence of holiness. It isn't about babbling in prayer; it isn't about any particular activity, or about what we do. Holiness is the fruit of the gift of God's love: a life lived in the Spirit.

Another motto I would choose would be from Psalm 119: "Your word is a lamp for my feet, a light on my path (Ps 119:105). Some theologians have called us 'Hearers of the Word'. What they mean is that we are essentially designed to hear and respond to the Divine Word, Christ. It is by hearing and responding to the Word of God that we are fulfilled. The whole purpose of the prayer of *lectio divina* is to allow God's Word to speak to us and to transform us. By a prayerful reading and rereading of Scripture we cannot fail to move along the path of discipleship. If we open our hearts to the Word of God, then our lives will change. As Isaiah puts it, the Word cannot fail to achieve what it was sent to do. In John's Prologue we hear, "The Word became flesh" (Jn 1:14). In meditating upon Sacred Scripture we encounter and are radically changed by Christ himself.

One form of prayer that I find useful occasionally is to pray my own salvation history. Just as the ancient Israelites reflected upon God's saving presence in their history, so we too can, from time to time, sit and look back over our journey. Where has God led us? Where have we come from?

The call to holiness involves, most of all, an openness: openness to God's love, to his voice in Scripture and Tradition; openness and honesty about who we really are. To let the prayer of *lectio divina* really nourish us we need to stop and listen. We need to let the Word take seed in us, to let it grow and produce fruit in our lives. This book began with the invitation, come and see: an invitation to spend time with the Lord, and to find out what he offers. It finishes now with the suggestion, stop and listen: an appeal to recognise God's presence in our lives.

NOTES

1. C. S. Lewis, *The Great Divorce*, (Fount Paperbacks), HarperCollins Publishers Ltd., 1946, p. 8.
2. *Ibid.*, p. 63.
3. *See* Genesis 3:6-10 and Luke 22:41-44.